MASTERING DOCUMENTATION

MASTERING DOCUMENTATION
WITH DOCUMENT MASTERS FOR SYSTEM DEVELOPMENT, CONTROL, AND DELIVERY

Paula Bell

Charlotte Evans

WILEY

JOHN WILEY & SONS

New York   Chichester   Brisbane   Toronto   Singapore

Library of Congress Cataloging in Publication Data:

Bell, Paula
Mastering documentation with document masters for
system development, control, and delivery.

Bibliography: p.
1. Communication of technical information.
2. Technology — Documentation.   I. Evans, Charlotte.
II. Title.
T10.5.B45   1989   005.1'5   88-27646
ISBN 0-471-61497-1

Printed in the United States of America.

10 9 8 7 6 5 4 3 2 1   Rev.

90   02541

To DR. MEYER FREEDMAN
and
To MICHAEL W. EVANS

TECHNICAL PROSE IS ALMOST IMMORTAL.
—FREDERICK P. BROOKS, JR. *THE MYTHICAL MAN-MONTH*

PREFACE

An essential component of product development and project control involves the gathering, recording, and updating of all pertinent information for the people who need it: managers, developers, administrators, and ultimately, end-users. The documents in support of the Boeing 747 are said to weigh as much as the plane!

On most projects, the amount of documentation can be measured in inverse proportion to its usefulness when poundage outweighs common sense. Document usefulness, like the product itself, is directly dependent on the system used to control its quality.

If you are a project manager, a technical manager, a software engineer, or a technical writer, then this book provides an efficient tool for you to master software documentation, rather than letting it master you, including:

HOW TO organize project and product data.

HOW TO present data tailored to specific audiences as documents advance through developmental stages to final delivery.

HOW TO establish the continuing relationships between input from developers and the documents that will be needed by end-users.

HOW TO standardize, organize, and control documents with the systematic technique of Document Masters.

The Document Masters included as Chapters 5 through 18 of this book provide the outlines for a full set of documents needed from conception to delivery of your system. Each

Master contains the structure and introduction to each section, telling the writer what to include and the reader what to expect. You can fill in the sections with the indicated information or tailor the Masters to reflect company or Government requirements.

The Masters will make writing easier for you and reading easier for your document users.

MASTERING DOCUMENTATION consists of an introduction and five parts, organized according to the concerns of large system development projects:

> The *Introduction* discusses the communication strategies that produce complete, consistent documentation throughout the project.
>
> PART I, *Getting Started*, presents the Document Masters technique in terms of: the documentation processes throughout the project life-cycle; the Document Master Tree, which relates levels and types of information and users to the project cycles; information for tailoring documents to specific needs; global and local standardization models; and methods by which documentation is to be written, updated, distributed, and tracked.
>
> PART II, *Specifying the System*, consists of Masters for the system functional, performance, and resource support specifications.
>
> PART III, *Controlling the Project*, consists of Masters for organizational management plans and tracking procedures.
>
> PART IV, *Developing the System*, consists of Masters for design, implementation, integration, and test of the system under development.
>
> PART V, *Delivering the System*, consists of Masters for documents that accompany the system to its users.

Appendixes list basic punctuation rules, present a publication format checklist, and discuss acronyms and abbreviations.

The glossary defines terms used to describe the system and its documentation.

We have designed the Document Masters from years of experience in writing, editing, producing, and controlling documents for large development efforts. We thank all the managers, engineers, programmers, writers, and editors in hightech companies and Government agencies who have helped us to learn—the hard way. We hope this book will make it easier for you.

Morgan Hill, California   **PAULA BELL**
June, 1988   **CHARLOTTE EVANS**

CONTENTS

INTRODUCTION

Publications, especially those written in support of software, are more and more often being reviewed as part of the products they describe. Good publications contribute not only to the product image, but also to the company coffers by decreasing engineering maintenance and hot-line calls.[1]

Unfortunately, company efforts to improve their publications often fail because documentation is considered a nuisance rather than a tool. The more complex the project, the more valuable—and the more vital—documentation becomes.

A development project can be considered complex when one or more of the following is true:

- Twenty-five or more people work on the project, in any capacity.
- Two or more technical disciplines are involved.
- The product employs a new software, hardware, or process technology.
- Multiple models, versions, or configurations are to be developed.
- A quarter-million or more lines of code will be written, figured with fudge factor times two and Murphy's Law.
- The project requires eighteen months or more to complete, figured with fudge factor squared and Murphy's Law.
- The project staff numbers work in different locations.

More often than not, projects escalate in complexity. Including documentation considerations in the initial planning stages provides a hedge against having to further increase project complexity with people dedicated to documentation that should have been produced and delivered earlier.

In addition, in order to be effective, documentation must be complete and current throughout the software project. Effective documentation is largely the result of effective communication.

Everything possible should be done to promote continuous communication from product inception to completion so that the end product will include good documentation for the people who will be using it to operate, build, or maintain your product for their jobs or entertainment. Every member of the project communicates with the end-user, whether they interface with the latest WYSIWYG (what you see is what you get) desktop publishing system, provide information for others to write, or track documentation from first memo to first customer ship.

The amount of information that is actually "common knowledge" on a project is frighteningly small. Any bit of information—including the name of the product—is less dependable with each day that passes because there is always more information, and the information is continually augmented, updated, and seen in new contexts.

No one can keep track of all the changes, as some people participate in meetings that decide small or large product issues while others concentrate on their particular part of the project, go on vacation, miss a meeting, take time off for an illness or celebration, are reorganized, or are replaced by new people.

As is true of the success of most company projects, good communication and its impetus must come from the top. **Executives** must be convinced that professional publications are significant to the quality of the company's image and must transmit that conviction to the people who can contribute throughout the project.

Management time spent in defining the interactions between people is as important as time spent in defining the interfaces of the product. Though no one wants to compromise the final publications because of untested information or inadequate time for editing, too many managers fail to see beyond the traditional divisions of product development organizations and support organizations. Project, program, and departmental managers who consider all facets of product success include documentation and its control in their plans from the blank page to the last minute release notes.

> If one examines the genealogy of a customer manual for a piece of hardware or software, one can trace not only the ideas, but also many of the very sentences and paragraphs back to the first memoranda proposing the product or explaining the first design.[2]

Discussions about the kinds and numbers of documents that the product will require should start with the initial planning of the project. The people who directly and indirectly contribute to document effectiveness must be encouraged to negotiate at all stages of the product life-cycle.

Ideally, a **document controller** is made part of the team as soon as product specifications are called for. The controller's job is to track the documentation through the phases of the life-cycle, to guard its integrity, and to make it accessible to those who need it. A good controller understands how to control multiple levels of details, and likes to.

The **technologists**, whether software or hardware oriented, supply the technical information and review its validity. Some technical types have written not only technical articles, but everything from poetry to science fiction. These people are to be encouraged, as their inputs generally need only light editing and clarification. However, the scope of their contributions should not expand to the detriment of their technical tasks. Other technical developers love word games, such as:

I R I E I A I D I I I N I G I

However, end-users hate reading between the lines, and they are the final judge of the success of the documentation.

Though a few technical people are superb writers, most are not. Managers who assign product development personnel to documentation tasks run the risk of second rate publications at the expense of full-time development, especially when engineers who think they are writers are not, and engineers who don't want to write are forced to.

> The users have a right to expect that the documentation be done as professionally as the programming. And considering the matter coolly, there is no reason to believe that a professional programmer will be qualified as a professional documenter . . . if documentation is elevated to a professional status all its own, so that the documenter can work side by side with the programmer without being made to feel inferior, we have the right to hope that documentation will improve.[3]

Technical writers should begin, at least on a part time basis, with the product specifications, and contribute to top-level design documents. Though it is possible that having writers get close to a product design can sometimes compromise their view of what the end-users will need to know, the risk is negligible when compared with the benefits of their understanding how the product is to be made to work.

Good communication with the **computer operations** department is critical on every project, but especially so when documentation is produced on a network that is shared throughout the company. Also, the system administrators, who keep the company's systems running, must have an understanding of how the text editors and formatters on their computers work in order to help tailor automated writing tools and to troubleshoot the inherent or resultant bugs. Systems administration and documentation personnel who meet regularly can keep both automated and human systems running with fewer glitches.

Coordinating **training** material development with documentation development can only improve both, as they share the common goal of teaching something that someone needs to know. The training and documentation personnel can share the workload, too, expecially in development of concepts and illustrations. It's essential that they share a common dictionary of terminology. The more that the manuals support the training for reference, the more that training can help end-users recall the information in the manuals.

On every development project, **everyone** must compete for the most limited of resources—other people's time. Setting up communication channels at the project's inception and keeping them open throughout its life improves not only the quality of the product and the quality of the documentation, but also the quality of life on the job.

PART 1
GETTING STARTED

Fifteen years after *The Mythical Man-Month*, Frederick Brooks writes, "The very nature of software makes it unlikely that there will be any . . . inventions that will do for software productivity, reliability, and simplicity what electronics, transistors, and large-scale integration did for computer hardware."[4]

Michael Evans agrees that "the reality is that software development is still, in a large part, a technical art form."[5]

Because of the nature of software, reality requires good documentation as the baseline to both software development and use.

It is not just the end-user of the product who can benefit from good documentation, but the entire project structure. "Software documents are written not just to be well organized and properly formatted, but also used by people who are trying to understand how a system works, its capabilities and limitations, and how and where to modify it."[6]

Documentation is the tool to develop and track the concepts, data structures, and interfaces that define a software project, from start to completion.

This part describes how to use the tool:

Chapter 1, Document Masters, describes the Document Masters technique in terms of documentation planning via the life-cycle model and document execution via the Master outlines provided in Parts II, III, IV, and V of this book.

Chapter 2, Document Tailoring, describes how to tailor the Document Masters to your specific needs, including document adaptation, contraction, decomposition, integration, and automation tools and techniques.

Chapter 3, Document Standards, describes both top down and bottom up approaches to standards for the front matter, back matter, and sections of all documentation in general and end-user documents in particular.

Chapter 4, Documentation Procedures, describes policies and procedures for scheduling documentation, establishing internal and external document control, generating drafts, getting and giving reviews, and producing end-user publications through multiple releases.

1 Document Masters

Though most participants view their projects as beyond state-of-the-art, something that has never been done before, in reality, projects that are to result in electronics-based products all share common properties. Rather than reinventing the wheel for each development project, you can use Document Masters to replace or significantly enhance the capability of the systems you now use to produce documentation.

The Document Masters provide not only the baselines needed to track the progress of the product from specification to delivery, but also the consistency that helps writers to explain concepts and readers to understand them. They incorporate the findings of the latest research in organizational and writing techniques that allow readers to learn and remember information.[7]

The Masters provided as Chapters 5 through 18 are divided into four major project activities:

■ Specifying the system to be developed.
■ Controlling the project.
■ Developing and testing the system according to specifications and controls.
■ Delivering the completed system.

In addition to these four major activities, Document

Masters can be classified according to a life-cycle model and a hierarchy tree.

LIFE-CYCLE MODEL

Permutations of the life-cycle model are almost universally used by project development teams. It is the best model we have, and it seems to map pretty well to reality.

Each phase of the life cycle must be accompanied by one or more formal documents, which are reviewed with any software resulting from that phase and which govern subsequent phases.[8]

Table 1–1 lists the phases of the life cycle and the

Table 1–1. Life-Cycle & Masters Correlation

LIFE-CYCLE PHASE	DOCUMENT MASTERS
Requirements Specification	System Requirements Specification Resource Requirements Specification
Project Control Structuring	Management Plan Engineering Change Proposal

System Development
  Architectural Design
  Prototype Design
  Detailed Design & Implementation
  Test Specification
  Test Implementation
	
	Architecture Design Document
	Prototype Design Document
	Detailed Design Document
	
	Test Specifications
	Test Reports

System Delivery	Users Guide Release Description System Administrators Guide Reference Guide Acceptance Signoff

Document Masters that are an integral part of each. As with any model of a complex system, the life-cycle is a simplified, idealized formalism for representing relationships among overlapping and iterative activities. Documentation that evolves through the repetitions of design phases, the sudden shifts because of technical difficulties, the reworking of nonworking features, the multiple reversals, large and small, is all the better for being a part of the process.

The following sections describe the idealized life-cycle phases and the ideal documents for each.

Requirements Specification Phase

A basic human impulse precedes and underlies each technological development.[9] The basic human impulse of technologists is to invent a system to do useful work. In order to implement the invention, it is necessary to specify the goals of the system and the resources it will take to achieve those goals.

A system's goals are expressed in terms of intended system functions; expected system performance, whether measured in MIPS, microns, or malleability; human and technological interfaces with which the system must be compatible; and other requirements dependent on system use, like front-end databasing or high security. Specifications, therefore, state system requirements in terms of:

Outputs it must produce. The outputs are really what the system is all about. And outputs are subject to both human and technological constraints, including customer acceptance (for example, the latest popup graphics); format constraints, which depend on the medium of communication (for example, online help displays or user guide page layout); established company and technical protocols and procedures (both stated and unstated); and special legal or security requirements.

Inputs it must accept. The inputs are subject to the same human and technological constraints as the outputs.

Operations it must perform. The operations are what happens between the input and the output. Operations will not be performed by the new system in exactly the same manner, sequence, or amount as in the old system, so the performance characteristics should specify the improvements over currently available systems—otherwise, why build a new one?

Resources it must have available. Resources include the people, time, tools, and facilities that the new system will require for development, installation, and continued operation. Have you ever worked on a development team that did not believe it would be easier to install the system than it actually turned out to be?

A product cannot be better than the *System Requirements Specification* written for it, and the specifications cannot be better than the analysis that goes into their creation.

The first step is to analyze the existing workload in terms of end-user applications. The second step is to evaluate the ways in which the workload will change and/or grow. These evaluations are generally based on mathematical analysis models. In short, systems analysis includes identification and specification of the following systems attributes:[10]

1. Purpose.
2. Components and the interrelationships among them.
3. Constraints that will be imposed by the environment.
4. Inputs and outputs that will be required.

Though technological excellence may be called for in the *System Requirements Specification*, the success of its accomplishment is controlled by the resources dedicated to it. The *Resource Requirements Specification* must enumerate the means to the end system in terms of each phase in the life-cycle and the skills, time, and equipment it will take to accomplish each.

The technical planners who write the requirements

specifications should include at least one user representative, one systems analyst, and one project tracker. To determine the requirements, they can ask the following questions:

What must the system do to become a useful product? If it's to be a new payroll system, it will still have to produce checks.

What might the system do in the future? It may not produce the checks directly but send the information to a bank by tape or electronic communication.

What performance level does the system have to meet? In other words, how is the system to be evaluated? It might have to improve transaction response time by half or process a greater variety of checks. The proposed users have the biggest say here, and their representative is often a marketeer.

How is the system to be supported with required resources throughout its life-cycle? Support requirements change with each phase, and, like the *System Requirements Specification*, the *Resource Requirements Specification* should be tracked and updated through the entire life-cycle.

Once the technical questions are addressed and the support resources assessed, the information must be communicated to project management for cost, schedule, and organizational assignment and control, and to the development team for decomposition through the phases of the design.

The specifications should also contain an executive summary for high-level decisions.

Project Control Structuring Phase

"The companies that we have called excellent are among the best at getting the numbers, analyzing, and solving problems with them."[11]

Control structuring requires planning and assignment of responsibility for management of system resources, configurations, and quality, and their inevitable parameter changes throughout the remaining phases of the project.

First, there is the hierarchical requirement. Complex tasks must be divided into parts that can be performed by individuals or groups. These individuals or groups must be coordinated if the larger task is to be completed successfully. If there are a large number of coordinators, they require coordination, and so on. Out of this hierarchy arise levels of authority, which are essential for the effective organization of a large number of interdependent tasks.

Second, there is the democratic requirement. In a democracy no individual may be subjected to the control of another who is not subject to control by those over whom he has some control.[12]

Though "treating people—not money, machines, or minds—as the natural resource may be the key to it all,"[13] management must take all possible views of the goals and resources, incorporate these views in a comprehensive *Management Plan*, and provide formal mechanisms for changing this plan.

The following figures illustrate some high-level views from various perspectives. The *Management Plan* must describe each view in detail.

Figure 1–1 is a hierarchy chart illustrating a management view of a multiproduct project.

Figure 1–2 is an interface diagram illustrating a management view of the project in terms of the project organizational units.

Figure 1–3 is a milestone chart illustrating a management view of the project as a series of milestone events.

Figure 1–4 is a costing sheet illustrating a management view of the project as a matter of dollars and cents.

Though management plans are predicated on a stable environment and requirements, good management means being ready for personnel, equipment, schedules, and any combination thereof to change at any time. Sometimes, if the project is small enough, and the company is on a roll, the product actually goes out on time and almost in budget. Plan for it, but don't count on it.

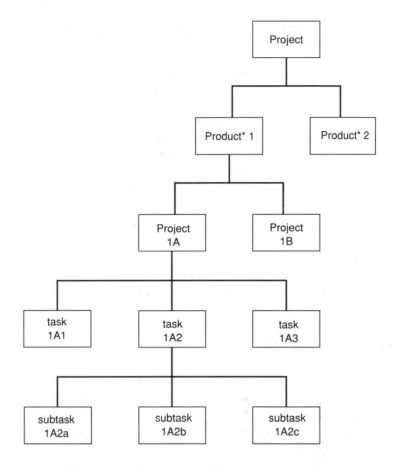

* = A project output that can be listed as a line item on a sales sheet, including system subsets, options, and platforms.

Figure 1–1 Project Hierarchy

Only rarely do members have self-contained tasks; in most cases, others possess critical information and expertise. Assistance from others is often required to implement decisions and programs. Difficulties with adequate coordination are compounded by a never-ending stream of externally induced changes. Policies, procedures, and regulations must be frequently modified in response to changes in tasks, technologies, and clients' needs. Thus, previously arranged modes of cooperation and past practices rapidly become obsolete.

Departments that strive for excellence have to develop methods to handle this high degree of interdependencies and increasing rate of change. Successful departments must be quickly responsive to new conditions and be able to untangle swiftly the snarls that inevitably develop when strong, capable individuals have to integrate their efforts.[14]

Putting change control mechanisms in place along with the management plans anticipates interactions and modifications that will occur throughout the software engineering development phases and that can be made for the full life-cycle of the system.

The *Engineering Change Proposal* is the official request and validation of any changes that will influence the development and/or delivery of the system.

System Development Phase

The engineers, programmers, and managers involved in system development might number in the thousands. As with any endeavor that brings together a great many people, the traditional principles obtain. One succinct list calls them out as the following:[15]

1. Goals and objectives that are challenging, clearly stated, and understood by everyone.
2. Clear and consistent communication, both top-down and bottom-up.
3. Motivation by opportunities for personal development and recognition.
4. Integration of ideas and standardization of good traits of previous, proven design successes.
5. Emphasis on results, and rewards that go along with them.

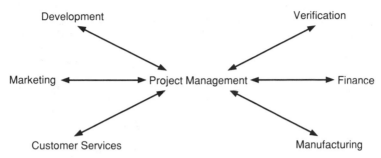

Figure 1–2 Project Organizational Interfaces

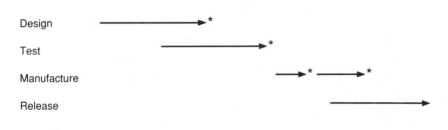

* = Management approval checkpoint

Figure 1–3 Milestone Chart

MANUFACTURING	UNIT COST	UNITS REQUIRED	TOTAL UNIT COST
Platform A Platform B TK50 tapes Reel tapes Personnel / hr. . .	$	$	$

TOTAL COST: $

Figure 1–4 Costing Sheet

6. Formal design reviews as accountability for performance and results.
7. Involvement by all concerned to ensure realistic cost and schedule parameters, analyze risks, and provide for contingencies.

Mom and apple pie, right? We've all heard it before, but you know from your own or others' experiences that projects not only espousing, but also following, these basic seven principles have a better chance to succeed—and to provide satisfaction to the tens or hundreds or thousands of people who will be working on the project before its completion.

Satisfaction is what keeps designers on the job, and having to replace designers mid or late in the project can result in potentially disastrous effects on a design. But even the best design environment won't keep everyone on the job, as software engineers are valuable resources in many industries. Good, timely documentation is therefore vital.

Most software engineers regularly work with sophisticated development and writing tools. If the documentation that accompanies those tools is sufficiently complete and clear, then the tool is that much more quickly accepted and productive. As end-users, they appreciate good documentation; but, like shoemakers, they forget that their own children need shoes too.

Because developers are often designing their part of the product independently, it is imperative that they document that part as they go along. It's equally imperative that the tests that prove each part against its functional specifications are documented independently.

> Separation of function is not to be despised, but neither should it be exalted. Separation is not an unbreakable law, but a convenience for overcoming inadequate human abilities, whether in science or engineering.[16]

The following sections describe separation of functions during the Development Phase in terms of:

1. Architectural design.
2. Prototyping.
3. Detailed design and implementation.
4. Test specification.
5. Test implementation.

Each of these subphases produces at least one document.

Architectural design

The ultimate object of design is form. The form is the solution to the problem; the context defines the problem. In other words, when we speak of design, the real object of discussion is not the form alone, but the ensemble comprising the form and its context.[17]

In still other words, it is not the logically independent forms of the input, output, and processing, but the way in which they work together in the context of the users' needs, that the architect must be concerned with.

Architecture design is the development of an effective solution to the *System Requirements Specification*. Tradeoffs are influenced within the context of system technology and performance, as well as the resources allocated in the *Management Plan*.

A systems architect answers the following basic questions to begin the design of a new system:[18]

1. How complete and efficient is the instruction set?
2. What data types and structures are directly and indirectly supported by the hardware?
3. What memory addressing modes are supported by the system?
4. How do system components communicate (hardware and software), and how is software synchronized with external events?

5. What design techniques are used to increase system performance?

6. What hardware and software protection facilities are available?

7. How are I/O devices supported by the system?

8. How flexible (easy to upgrade and modify) is the system architecture design?

9. What error detection or correction techniques are supported in the architecture?

Not RISC or CISC, nor centralized or distributed control, nor local or remote processing, nor any other solution is universally effective to meet all requirements. For example, there are many alternatives for handling input: tape, disk, optical character recognition, ink scanning devices, voice activation. Similarly, there are many ways to receive output: tape or disk files, terminal displays, hardcopy, voice. And, of course, there are multiple ways in which operations can be designed to accommodate the input and output functions: table lookup, calculation, decision tables, search algorithms, heuristics.

The design detail in the *Architecture Design Document* should present the functional architecture explicitly enough to direct further development. Approved architectural information can then be fed back to the management planners to update resource allocation and forwarded to prototyping or detailed design.

Prototyping

A prototype should be developed at the end of the architectural design so that anomalies and misunderstandings can surface before the detailed design and implementation has begun.

The larger the system, the more that prototyping will enhance design and implementation. Prototypes can be used:[19]

1. *To demonstrate the user interface.* The demonstration prototype acts as a temporary implementation in order to illustrate the displays and controls for user acceptance of the system. Demonstration prototypes can also help developers find inadequacies in concept and consistency.

2. *To perform the operations.* The operating prototype actually processes data, but often as an inelegant solution to demonstrate functional capabilities at the user interface.

3. *To model machine performance for comparisons* of design alternatives for problem areas in the architecture. A performance prototype might be built to model response times, memory requirements, transaction parameters, database storage and retrieval, or communications. As the models are generally very incomplete, performance prototypes are generally discarded once a design has been decided on, and require only brief documentation that describes how the model was built and its results.

4. *To begin development of the full application.* The development prototype must certainly be fully documented through all phases of design and implementation, as it is the eventual implementation of the application.

The first two prototypes, coded just for show or for quick and dirty operations, can cause severe design problems when they become the beginning of the actual system.

Some of the more visible interfaces, such as help and query facilities, could lead a user to believe that the prototype is meeting the requirements; however, the prototype of the outer shell is not the prototype of the system.[20]

For all but the performance prototype, then, documentation must include detailed descriptions of the design and implementation.

And not only the system can be prototyped. The documents themselves can also benefit from prototyping during their development. In this case, prototyping involves a systematic attempt to use feedback in resolving uncertain documentation requirements by presenting sample users with working documentation and rapidly revising and enhancing the documentation as a result of progressive user/documenter understanding of the documentation requirements. Prototyping provides a vehicle for reader involvement and commitment to the documentation process and could result in higher evaluations of the resulting documentation and the documentation process. Furthermore, the presentation of documentation with application system prototypes can contribute to better understanding of the prototype and thus stimulate effective system feedback.[21]

Detailed design and implementation

Detailed design and implementation is the heart, the meat, and the sweat of the development project.

During the Detailed Design and Implementation Phase, the system architect is first joined by software gurus and technical team leaders. The team leaders take responsibility for subsystems within the product system and assign technical staff to their design and implementation. All design activities must be accompanied by regularly scheduled inputs to the *Detailed Design Document*.

System implementation necessarily implies design changes. Though general user requirements as set forth in the *System Requirements Specification* tend to remain in force, a requirement can generally be implemented in several ways, subtly or dramatically changing the original intent. Some architectural descriptions no longer apply as more details and more complexities are incurred. The resources actually available and the real progress of the design to date are also strong influences as the design progresses.

All changes should be documented and approved via an

Engineering Change Proposal and reflected in the *Detailed Design Document.*

Design and implementation should imply reviews at all levels—coding practices, coded unit, integrated module, and full system—before the development unit, module, or system is formally tested. This approach stresses incremental checks on design progress.

The incremental development approach means that after the top-down designs are defined, the detailed design of a group of units is begun in priority order and dependency. After the detailed design of a unit is complete and documented, coding for that unit is begun; after a group of interdependent units is coded and tested, they are combined into a module.

Coding units and modules independently allows an incremental version of the system to run even before all designs are completed, which offers several advantages.

> In our case, the incremental development approach resulted in the availability of an early version of the system, which had a big morale-boosting effect on both the team and management. It also had the effect of spreading the system integration work load over time. In fact, the capability of doing unit and partial integration testing on the host prior to the target system resulted in substantial improvements in programmer productivity.[22]

As complexity, iteration, and incremental design all influence good documentation, it is best to assign document sections to specific units and modules; relegating detailed information to appendixes adds to the chance for oversights as the document is updated.

Test specification

In order for formal testing to be adequate to the task at hand, test development should begin almost immediately after detailed design, using the information in the *System Requirements Specification*, the verification portions of the *Management Plan*, and the *Architecture Design Document*. These documents determine the initial criteria against which the *Test Specifications* is to be written. As the *Detailed Design Document* is written and updated, its contents should be considered in detailed test specifications.

Test specifications include tests to evaluate:[23]

Standardization of system displays and user inputs. These tests should ensure that the system presents a consistent user view.

Program interaction between asynchronous components. These tests can include simulation first in a standalone configuration and then be repeated in an integrated subsystem.

System interactions between system, software subsystem, and data components. These tests should execute each test component individually and then in increasingly more complete configurations.

Equipment interaction between individual system components in a network. These tests of data and control exchanges should be simulated at first and then repeated with hardware. If the system is to run on multiple platforms, then the *Test Specifications* must include platform-dependent tests.

Recoverability, or fallback, from hardware or software failure. These tests should ensure that the programs can be continued from some checkpoint, that files are not damaged, and that the entire recovery process can be performed in a reasonable amount of time.

Overload for all tables, buffers, queues, or other storage areas. These tests should fill all memory constructs up to and beyond their capacity to test for data integrity and recovery.

Each test should be designed for repeatability and reproducibility: **Repeatability** because of differences in timing, whereby the same sequence of test case inputs, phased slightly differently or executing in a different configuration or under different loading conditions, can result in different outputs or execution characteristics. **Reproducibility** so that in the event of a failure, the exact environment and test conditions can be achievable and any failures recreatable for all test cases, particularly in a real time environment.

Test specification requirements include criteria that will define a passing status for each type of test, the methods to prove the criteria, and the procedures by which the components are to be tested.

Criteria are measurable effects that establish the degree to which a component satisfies the expectations of the test.

Methods include demonstration, measurement, simulation, and data gathering and analysis techniques that will be used to test the components against the criteria.

Procedures cover resources necessary to carry out the tests, specific inputs or test cases to be supplied, and actions to be taken according to test performance. Procedures are influenced by the consideration for validity so that when units are tested as components of modules, and modules of subsystems and so forth up to full system level, earlier tests are not invalidated, and all components involved in the current test meet their combined criteria.

Test implementation

Test and integration tasks represent the bottom line of the software development process. The activities during this project period are the means by which design integrity is verified, traceability to requirements validated, and operational integrity established.[24]

During test execution, the primary categories of errors will include the following:[25]

Test case errors: Whenever an erroneous result occurs, the test case should be checked first.

Logic errors: Most testing efforts find logic errors. If a test input exposes the presence of a bug, then the same input should always be presented a second time, and the record should show whether the same bug manifested itself in the same way.

Timing errors: Timing errors cannot be easily repeated as they are often a function of coincidental combinations of events within the program not anticipated in the *Test Specifications*.

Throughput and capacity errors: These errors are evidence of unacceptable performance of the program. Though the software generates the correct output, it takes too much time, uses an exorbitant amount of memory, or hangs.

Vendor system errors: If the system testing involves vendor hardware and/or software, then errors tracked to vendor products should be negotiated according to company protocols.

Documentation errors: If a documentation error prevents the user from using the system, then it is as serious as an operational error.

   Test Specifications are followed for the test of each unit, module, subsystem, and the completed system. The *Test Report* contains the descriptions of each test in terms of resources and procedures used to carry out the test, the method used to prove the criteria, the results of the test based on those criteria, and recommendations where test results are anomalous.

   Each error that results in a failed test must be logged in the *Test Report* and dealt with before the product is delivered. The errors that are critical must, of course, be tracked to their source and eliminated. If the error has been shown to be the result of vendor software or hardware, then negotiations with the vendor must be initiated. If the error is deemed noncritical or a temporary workaround is found, then the error and workaround can be described in the *Release Description* on system delivery.

SYSTEM DELIVERY PHASE

The delivery of very large software products is often incremental, scheduled in Alpha, Beta, and Production releases.

Customers accepting Alpha release versions of the system should expect to find bugs and to help fix them by submitting detailed reports.

Beta software releases incorporate fixes from the Alpha release and, usually, additional system features. Along with the customers who accepted the Alpha version, additional customers may accept the Beta version of the software.

Once the Beta fixes have been made, the software becomes Production worthy.

The delivery documents must be in sync with the releases: If there are Alpha and Beta versions, then all the end-user documentation—also in Alpha or Beta status—must accompany them. As changes are made to the product, these changes must be incorporated in the publications.

The Production version of the publications are the culmination of the documentation effort that began with the specification of the system.

Every system requires a *Users Guide* that explains the system in terms of how to perform the tasks it addresses.

Every release of the system, from the Alpha version to the last enhancement, requires a *Release Description* that describes the system in terms of new features, known problems and workarounds, and installation procedures.

If the system will require special data, access, or resource allocation from the operating system and/or hardware, then a *System Administrators Guide* is necessary.

If the end-user of the system will be maintaining or modifying the software, then a *Reference Guide* is necessary.

Very large systems generally require a pre-negotiated signoff of acceptance, especially when they are built to Government specifications or to control critical or hazardous operations. The *Acceptance Signoff* accompanies the delivered system and contains or refers to an approved acceptance agreement. It is the document for official signoff by the customer.

DOCUMENT MASTER TREE

Figure 1–5, the Document Master Tree, illustrates the hierarchical dependencies of the Masters.

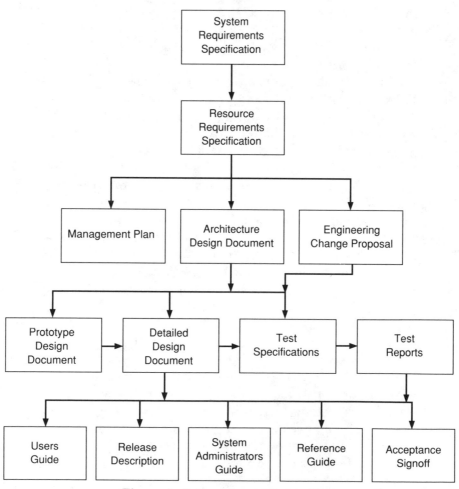

Figure 1–5 Document Master Tree

Top-down, the product germinates from the *System Requirements Specification*. As each level is decomposed to lower levels, design information becomes more detailed. But data must also be sent bottom-up until the latest information is reflected in the topmost applicable node. For example, if a design decision or resource constraint changes at the unit level, then the influences of the change must also be summarized in higher-level system design document sections.

Each Document Master illustrated in the tree is provided in Chapters 5 through 18. Each includes:

■ The table of contents for the document.

■ Section and subsection headers.

■ Introductory material in each section and subsection.

■ Suggestions for tables and figures.

■ Indication of information that the writer is to supply.

The sections and subsections of the Document Master may be thought of as patterns, or **templates**. Some templates are **boilerplate**; that is, it is not necessary to modify their contents at all. Boilerplates generally introduce topics that are to be discussed in sections immediately following. Figure 1–6 illustrates the boilerplate for Section 4 of the *Release Description*.

4. KNOWN PROBLEMS & WORKAROUNDS

The following are known problems and their workarounds. Fixes will be supplied as they become available.

Figure 1–6 Document Master Boilerplate

Some templates are used globally (across multiple documents); others, locally (specific to one document).

Figure 1–7 illustrates the global template for Section 1 of the Masters provided in Parts II, III, and IV.

Figure 1–8 illustrates the template local to Section 6.1 of the *System Requirements Specification*.

Figure 1–9 illustrates a filled-in template for the preface in the *Users Guide*.

1. SCOPE

The following subsections describe the scope of this [SYSTEM ID] [DOCUMENT NAME] in terms of its purpose, audience, organization, and applicable documents.

1.1 PURPOSE

This [DOCUMENT NAME] provides information for [DOCUMENT PURPOSE DESCRIBED IN TERMS OF USER TASKS].

1.2 AUDIENCE

The intended users of this [DOCUMENT NAME] are [USER TITLES] (with [PREREQ-UISITE KNOWLEDGE]).

1.3 ORGANIZATION

This [DOCUMENT NAME] describes
[DOCUMENT ORGANIZATION DESCRIPTION]

1.4 APPLICABLE DOCUMENTS

The following documents provide information necessary to understanding this [DOCU-MENT NAME].

[LIST OF APPLICABLE DOCUMENTS]

Figure 1–7 Document Master Global Template

NOTE that the information you fill in is indicated by square brackets [ ] throughout the Masters, and optional information is indicated by parentheses ( ). Variable numbers are indicated by n; the n always produces at least two iterations of the section.

6.1 GENERAL TEST REQUIREMENTS

The following test methods will be used to verify that the system requirements have been satisfied.

1. Demonstration. Observable functional operation of the system (or some part of the system) not requiring the use of special instrumentation or test equipment.
2. Data Recording and Analysis. Operation of the system (or some part of the system) and collection and subsequent, observations, interpretations, and extrapolations made from the data.

n. [ADDITIONAL TEST METHOD].
[ADDITIONAL TEST METHOD DESCRIPTION]

Figure 1–8 Local Template

PREFACE

The following describes this document in terms of purpose, audience, organization, and related documentation.

PURPOSE

This *Fastrack Users Guide* provides information and procedures to use on the Fastrack System.

AUDIENCE

The intended users of this guide are disk drive designers with knowledge of the 2901 interface protocols. UNIX knowledge is helpful.

ORGANIZATION

This guide describes Fastrack in terms of:

1. Design entry
2. Design validation
3. Design modification

DOCUMENTATION

Related documentation includes:

Fastrack Simulation Users Guide

Fastrack Test Generation Users Guide

Figure 1–9 Filled-In Template

2 Document Tailoring

The requirement of the market, the size of the development project, the company culture, and the available resources dictate the requirements for system documentation. You can tailor the Document Masters to meet your particular needs in terms of:

- Adaptation to product specifications.
- Contraction for simple projects.
- Decomposition for complex projects.
- Integration with existing systems.
- Automation to take advantage of computerized writing aids.

The following sections describe these options.

ADAPTATION

The system that is the goal of your project determines the information that forms the contents of its documentation and the terminology used to describe its functions. For example, Table 2–1 lists the differences between batch and online system descriptors.[26] End-user publications, especially, vary dramatically depending on product specifications, so their Masters are apt to change the most.

Table 2–1. Batch and Online Descriptors

BATCH	ONLINE
Pre-processing	Transaction logic
Keypunch instructions	Man-machine dialogue
Program flowcharts	Screen formats
File definitions	Input codes
Record layouts	Command syntax
Program documentation	Module documentation
Console operator documentation (run book)	Data base organization
Input forms	Data base access methods
Output forms	Communications queues
Report distribution lists	Security tables
	Communications line control
	File directories
	Communication network layouts
	Terminal specification
	Terminal operator instructions
	Transaction logs
	Linkage records

CONTRACTION

The full set of Document Masters can be contracted by combining Masters or by deleting sections or full documents.

If the project is estimated at less than six months, or if the product is fairly simple, then you might want to combine the Masters, as illustrated in Figure 2–1.

If your product does not require all the information outlined in the Masters, then, rather than deleting sections, you can input N/A after section headers that are not applicable. The N/A sections will thereby state that the information is not part of the project.

If your project does not follow the whole life-cycle (for example, if the architecture is an established standard like the 1750 instruction set, or the language is an unmodified standard like Ada), then a reference to the applicable

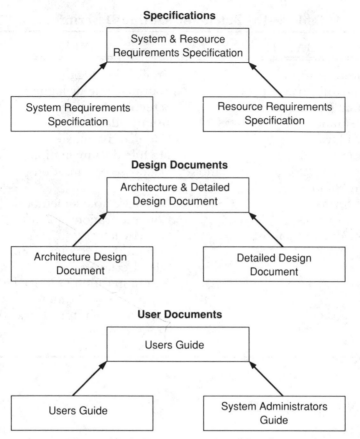

Figure 2–1 Document Combination

document in the *Detailed Design Document* is all that is necessary.

However, addressing all Masters motivates project participants to review the current information and thereby begin from a mutual baseline of understanding.

DECOMPOSITION

The Masters can be decomposed into additional independent documents for projects of considerable size or systems of high complexity. For example, the *Management Plan* can be decomposed into separate documents for each of the functional groups, and the plans for functional subgroups can be further decomposed, as illustrated in Figure 2–2.

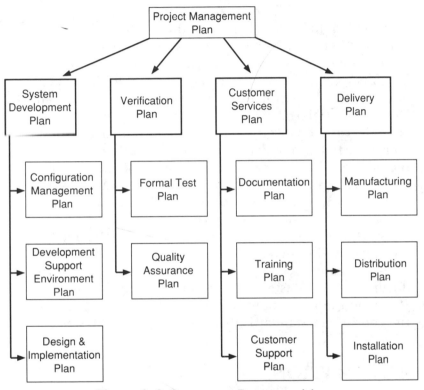

Figure 2–2 Document Decomposition

The lower-level plans should then be referenced and summarized in the top-level *Project Management Plan*.

INTEGRATION

Documentation is neither conceived nor delivered in a vacuum, so you might be obliged to integrate the Masters with an already established company organization or set of documents.

If your project will be carried out according to an already established organizational structure, then the set of Masters in Part III can serve to reorganize and/or sharpen descriptions in the standard documents.

If your documentation must conform to an existing set of Government or company regulation documents, then you can use the Masters as a guide to introducing the information and to double check that all the information is adequately covered. The Masters will map one-to-many or many-to-one in the set you are using; for example, Table 2–2 lists four major activity categories of the Masters correlated to the Department of Defense (DoD) Data Item Description (DID) 2167A.

In the case of Government document standards, although you must follow the agency's outline exactly, you can use the Masters to incorporate consistency standards—for example, beginning introductions to each section by "The following . . . "; and if the whole section is introductory, providing lists of subsections that immediately follow. Following the consistency standards helps readers to anticipate and understand the information.

In the case of integration with company established documents, the Masters may require the addition of sections. If you add more sections to the Masters, then, again, follow the consistency standards that are part of the Masters.

AUTOMATION

Documentation, like all disciplines involved in system development, has profited from computerized automation. It is surprising that many software development companies are still unaware or not convinced of its variety and usefulness.

Using a computer to help design a computer is not new. Since the advent of MSI (medium scale integration), no human or team of humans could manually design the transistors, circuits, and logic on a board or a chip in a competitive timeframe. Design automation (DA), or computer aided design (CAD), started in the late '60s. Now, hardware offerings from companies like Sun and Apollo are cranking out designs with MIPS produced only by

Table 2-2. Document Correlation

DEPARTMENT OF DEFENSE 2167A	DOCUMENT MASTERS
Software Product Specification	System Requirements Specification
Computer Resources Integrated Support Document	Resource Requirements Specification
Software Quality Program Plan (2168)	Management Plan
	Engineering Change Proposal
	Architecture Design Document
System/Segment Design Document	Prototype Design Document
	Detailed Design Document
Software Design Document	Test Specifications
Software Test Description	Test Reports
Software Test Report	Users Guide
Software User's Manual	Release Description
Version Description Document	System Administrators Guide
	Reference Guide
Software Programmer's Manual	Acceptance Signoff
System/Segment Specification	
Interface Requirements Specification	
Software Requirements Specification	
Software Development Plan	
Software Test Plan	
Interface Design Document	
Computer System Operator's Manual	
Firmware Support Manual	

31

mainframes a few years ago. And software offerings by companies including Mentor and Silicon Compiler Systems provide design entry, analysis, validation, and tapeout functions.

Computer aided software engineering (CASE), as an idea, has also been around since the '60s, but has not progressed as far or as fast, because of the nonphysical, conceptual aspect of software and the diversity by which concepts can be interpreted and implemented. However, recent products like Lisp machines from Symbolics and POWER from Expertware are being used by software development engineering staffs to develop and test system and applications software.

Using a computer to help with documentation also began in the '60s when IBM put primitive word processing on the Magnetic Tape/Selectric Composer System in 1964. By 1981, the Xerox Star System, the first WYSIWYG, could merge text and graphics using icons and a mouse. In 1983, Hewlett-Packard Corporation made laser printing part of desktop publishing with the LaserJet, and Apple produced the LaserWriter in 1985. In the same year, Abode Systems introduced PostScript, a device- and resolution-independent printer interface language that is fast becoming the standard.

So computer aided publishing (CAP) has enjoyed great popularity in the last half-dozen years, as automated text, graphics, and layout packages have allowed companies to produce documentation on a laser printer that would have required sophisticated, very expensive typesetting machinery just a decade ago. As workstations gain popularity, CAP systems are being designed and/or ported to big-screen, full-color, multi-MIP processors.

The following describes the tools and the techniques you can use to automate documentation and the Masters.

TOOLS

In the simplest kind of desktop publishing, one person "does it all" (at least by implication). But, in fact, better than 95%

of all publishing involves a division of labor among people with quite different professional and business aptitudes, training, and skills. These include editorial planning/direction, content research, writing, editing, visual design, illustration, various pre-press production activities, reproduction, binding, packaging, warehousing, order fulfillment, and shipping.[27]

Automated tools have evolved in the areas of inputting, manipulating, and outputting textual information by making use of various kinds of programs to accomplish these text processing tasks, including editors, formatters, and wordprocessors.

A text editor allows you to enter, change, move, copy, delete, and save text interactively on the screen. IBM mainframes run the CMS and SPF editors under the VM and MVS operating systems, respectively. DEC machines run EDIT under VMS, and under UNIX editors include ed, ned, Emacs, and vi.

A text **formatter** requires you to explicitly direct an electronic printer or typesetter for page layout, type font and size, and so on by entering format commands along with the text. Formatters are often effectively used by software developers, who are accustomed to learning new languages, to understanding the concepts of file storage and retrieval, and to keyboarding. Written by and for programmers, these systems often require quasi-programming skills, treating authors as programmer-typists.[28]

Figure 2–3 and 2–4 illustrate the input and output of one of the versions of the roff (runoff) formatter originally designed at Bell Laboratories.

A **wordprocessor** is a combination editor and formatter that generally requires significantly fewer formatting commands to be entered. They may be input along with text or by means of control keys that insert visible or invisible format control systems. "The biggest advantage of a wordprocessor over a typewriter is that it encourages writers to make changes because changes are so much easier to make, and, hopefully, will lead to better writing in general. In fact, early studies indicate that this is the case."[29,30]

```
.ce
.B "TROUBLESHOOTING"
.LP
.sp .5i
.LP
The following sections describe troubleshooting problems in terms of their:
.RS
.br
Symptoms(s)
.br
Cause(s)
.br
Solution(s)
.RE
.sp 3
.IP "\f3Symptom:\fP" 1.25i
Most or all of circuit outputs have the value "X" when a high or low
value was expected
.IP "\f3Cause:\fP" 1.25i
When automatic clock
toggle definitions are used in MicroSim; some test vectors contain
no clocking information
.IP "\f3Solution:\fP" 1.25i
Add clock definitions to the test vectors by adding
a clock toggle definition or by adding the clock signal to the
vector input field.
.LP
.sp 4
.IP "\f3Symptoms:\fP" 1.25i
The error message: "Name 'xxx' not found in circuit." is displayed.
.IP "\f3Causes:\fP" 1.25i
The sim2cir program has not been sourced OR
a signal name in the header of the test vector file does not match the
name of any signal in the EDIF circuit model.
.IP "\f3Solutions:\ fP" 1.25i
Source the sim2cir program AND/OR
look in the EDIF model to determine the names used for top level
signals, and change the test vector names to agree with the EDIF names.
```

Figure 2–3 roff Input

Wordprocessing programs are the nucleus of desktop publishing. WordPerfect, Microsoft Word, Multimate Advantage from Ashton Tate, and WordStar and Display Writer from MicroPro are just the top five of the plethora of packages that run under IBM DOS and its compatibles.

As desktop publishing systems proliferate, more tools are steadily incorporated or offered as compatible options.

For complicated formats or text that can be positioned around graphics, there are several **page layout** programs available. They are often patterned on PageMaker, an Aldus Corporation product which runs on the Macintosh, but have been developed for both stand-alone and networked

TROUBLESHOOTING

The following sections describe troubleshooting problems in terms of their:
   Symptom(s)
   Cause(s)
   Solution(s)

Symptom:	Most or all of circuit outputs have the value "X" when a high or low value was expected.
Cause:	When automatic clock toggle definitions are used in MicroSim; some test vectors contain no clocking information.
Solution:	Add clock definitions to the test vectors by adding a clock toggle definition or by adding the clock signal to the vector input field.

Symptom:	The error message: "Name 'xxx' not found in circuit." is displayed.
Causes:	The sim2cir program has not been sourced OR a signal name in the header of the test vector file does not match the name of any signal in the EDIF circuit model.
Solutions:	Source the sim2cir program AND/OR look in the EDIF model to determine the names used for top level signals, and change the test vector names to agree with the EDIF names.

Figure 2–4 roff Output

workstation platforms. The screen displays are exactly or pretty close to WYSIWYG.

Graphics packages offer libraries of predefined illustrations as well as the capability to modify them or create new original art. The Graphic Arts Department at Oak Ridge National Laboratory has been using computer-generated graphics since 1979 and has concluded that:

Computer graphics output can match manual work for publication graphics (so well, in fact, that a *C* had to be added to the drawing number to show that the work was done on the computer so that the artist knew where to look for the original archival copy) . . . . In addition, hidden goals were achieved: the computer graphics capability did not take needed work away from the manual group; instead a new service and growth area was created; and a large load of "drudge" work was lifted from the manual group, freeing them for more creative, satisfying work.[31]

Outliners have been developed and marketed as part of wordprocessing systems (WordPerfect and Microsoft Word, for example) or as a standalone product (Think Tank 512 and More from Living VideoText), but their value has yet to be formally assessed. A **table of contents generator**, however, is a critical form of outliner. Any automated text processing system for the creation of large documents should provide an easy method for automatically producing a table of contents, preferably without manual preprocessing, and with the capability of user modification.

Index generators are available to cut the tremendous time and chance for error involved in manual creation of indexes. Some automated indexers work on a list matching principle; others require key-coded marking in text. The less pre- and post-processing that an indexer needs, the easier it is to use. Also, the algorithms for assigning page numbers to the index entries are not always bug free, so you'll have to check up on the indexer by looking up a few of the entries, choosing words or phrases that appear at different locations on a page.

Spell checkers are a vital part of any text processing system. Most wordprocessors include spell checkers as part of the system, and most mainframe and network systems include spell check utilities. Computers were designed to take care of such tasks as hunting for misspellings or double entries of a word, and if they are not always more competent at the job, they're certainly faster.

A spell checker consults its list(s) of valid words and flags any word that does not appear on the list. Many spell checkers include a helpful prompt of correct spellings for invalid words, and most spell checkers include the capability to add words to the list. It is efficient to add the proper names and acronyms that are used to describe the system that you are documenting. Each proper name and acronym can be copied into a glossary file at the same time.

However, many words that are valid to the spell checker (on its list) are not valid in the context of the text, for example, "think" instead of "thing" or "work" instead of "word." In the first case, there are some very advanced spell checkers that consult syntax rules, so that "think," a verb, would not be acceptable in the place of "thing," a noun. The same is true of the many words that serve as both nouns and verbs, for example, using "contract" where "contact" was intended. In the case of "work" or "word," however, only very sophisticated, and still very limited, programs can make the distinction based on semantics (meaning). So before the final printing, the text must be read for semantic-spelling, preferably on hardcopy. Human eyes and minds are still the only devices that can make the infinite distinctions in natural language.

Style checkers, which check for grammar and syntax, are useful for a cursory comment on the overall readability of the text in terms of grade level and rhetorical structures.

Grade level assignment is generally determined by a fog index, which counts occurrences of syllables in a word and words in a sentence. None has yet been marketed specifically for technical prose.

Calculating rhetorical structure includes parsing then counting the types of sentences used (simple, compound, complex), deciding whether they are in active or passive voice, and determining their distribution in the text.

Some style checkers also make recommendations. For example, style checking on a 12-page double-spaced term paper produced 93 computer-generated suggestions for change and 20 advisor-generated suggestions for change. There was only one common suggestion, which was incorporated with 10 of the computer changes and 16 of the advisor changes.[32] Like software development, writing style is as much art as computation.

However, style checkers are far from failures, as they make writers more aware of the mechanics of writing. A study conducted at Bell Labs with The Writers Workbench, a style checker that runs under UNIX systems, found that after style checking and corrections, text contained fewer awkward constructions, including fewer passive sentences, and more awareness of grammar and punctuation in general.[33] It is almost impossible to work with a computer and not learn something new in the process.

Lancaster and Warner have cited significant advancements in the interactive generation of text, including collaborative authorship via electronic nets, the availability of databases in all areas and disciplines, and the transmission of text from origin of input to final form of output.[34]

Networking is ideal for collaboration. If you're working with another writer on a shared project, you can hold conferences on screen and brainstorm together—with the important advantage that all of your conversation becomes part of an electronic file in both of your systems. These on-screen exchanges can lead to the same kind of excitement and synergy that in-person meetings often do, and because the network conversations are written, you'll be exercising your writing muscles (mental and physical) as you think together.[35]

The latest capability—and its accompanying buzz word—is **hypertext**. Hypertext is driven by a database management system that controls data in a network of nodes connected by links. Each node contains user information. For example, if a node were displayed as a highlighted word in text on the screen, then selecting that word would cause the screen to display additional information about the concept or topic appropriate to that word.

> Hypertext electronic documents provide most of the flexibility of reference works as well as add a number of new features . . . . Each node can be thought of as analogous to a short section of an encyclopedia article or perhaps a graphic image with a brief explanation. The links join these sections to one another to form the article as a whole and the articles to form the encyclopedia. These links are usually shown for each node as a "from" link pointing to the node just read and a set of "to" links that indicate the (usual) multiple nodes which one may select to read next.

Thus one moves from node to node by selecting the desired "to" link, or the "from" link to return to the previous node.[36]

The even more flexible **hypermedia** nodes can contain not only text, but also complex graphics, audio, and video.

The decades-old concept is becoming an intriguing tool now that Apple's HyperCard is popularizing the software.

Though the hardware and software are certainly improving, the ambiguity and idiosyncrasies inherent in natural languages are exactly what computers do not excel at. Programming rules for the infinite possible ambiguous concatenations likes "time flies like the wind" and "fruit flies like bananas" is not an easy task. Computer scientists, cognitive scientists, and linguists are working in artificial intelligence (AI) labs both in academia and big business on problems like this.

Even automating **hyphenation**, whose rules are better understood than most formalities of written language, can get you in trouble. The story is told of a psychologist who sued the manufacturers of the hyphenation algorithm that printed his announcement as:

DR. STEVENSON THE - RAPIST OPENS CLINIC

Also, beware of "almost" compatibility in both hardware and software. As IBM and Apple products become the *de facto* standard, choosing add-ons and software designed specifically to their hardware and operating systems is a good bet.

The more that engineers and writers use the tools, the more aware they will be of what's still missing. Who better to improve the tools than the people who need them?

Techniques

The Document Masters lend themselves to computer automation. The level and complexity of automation you can achieve is dependent on the techniques you choose to implement.

At the operating system level, UNIX and DOS conveniently provide the hierarchical structure for placement of the Masters in directories, subdirectories, and files, corresponding to the Document Master Tree, as illustrated in Figure 2–5. The procedure to construct the filesystem is described in Chapter 4.

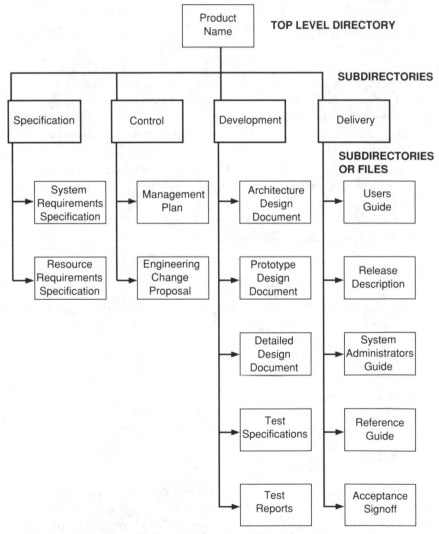

Figure 2–5 Project Masters Directory

Each document file can then contain the Document
Masters and the format commands. The format commands
you enter depend on the text processing system you are
using. The following two figures illustrate the commands
in Section 1 of the Masters for systems using Scribe and
WordStar.

Scribe (Figure 2–6), which runs under UNIX, is a registered trademark of Unilogic, Ltd. The @ symbol serves the

```
@make(books)
@style(stringMax 4000,
       spacing 1,
       leftmargin .75 inch,
       topmargin .80 inch,
       bottommargin .5 inch,
       indentation 0,
       spread 1)
@String[RevisionNumber="@value(date)"]
@Style(Justification Off)
@Style(DOUBLESIDED)
@pageheading(odd,
             right="@title(newchapter)")
@pageheading(even,
             left="@title(newchapter)")
@pagefooting(odd,
             right="@value(page)")
@pagefooting(even,
             left="@value(page)")
@comment [ End of the standard header  ]
@label{syspry}
@newpage
@chapter{SCOPE}
The following subsections describe the scope of this
[SYSTEM ID] [DOCUMENT NAME] in terms of its purpose,
audience, organization, and applicable documents.
@section{PURPOSE}
This [DOCUMENT NAME] provides information for [DOCUMENT
PURPOSE DESRCIPTION IN TERMS OF USER TASKS].
@section{AUDIENCE}
The intended users of this [DOCUMENT NAME] are [USER
TITLES] (with [PREREQUISITE KNOWLEDGE]).
@section {ORGANIZATION}
This [DOCUMENT NAME] describes
@begin (verbatim)
        [DOCUMENT ORGANIZATION DESCRIPTION].
@end (verbatim)
@section {APPLICABLE DOCUMENTS}
The following documents provide information necessary to
understanding this [DOCUMENT NAME].
@begin (itemize)
        [LIST OF APPLICABLE DOCUMENTS]
@end (itemize)
@newpage
@include(intro.mss)
@include(syscomm.mss)
@include(yai.mss)
```

Figure 2–6 Section 1 with Scribe Commands

same purpose as the dot (.) symbol in the roff formatter—to
make the program recognize one of its commands. Note the
setup commands at the head of the file. For long documents
it is convenient to put setup commands in a driver file, which
then contains commands to call and include individual files
of sections that follow.

WordStar (Figure 2–7), which runs under DOS, is a registered trademark of MicroPro International Corporation.
File and editing functions are specified by menu, by control
keys, and by dot commands.

```
^Bl. SCOPE^B

The following subsections describe the scope of this
[SYSTEM ID] [DOCUMENT NAME] in terms of its purpose,
audience, organization, and applicable documents.

^Bl.l PURPOSE^B

This [DOCUMENT NAME] provides information for [DOCUMENT
PURPOSE DESCRIBED IN TERMS OF USER TASKS].

^Bl.2 AUDIENCE^B

The intended users of this [DOCUMENT NAME] are [USER
TITLES] (with [PREREQUISITE KNOWLEDGE]).

^Bl.3 ORGANIZATION^B

This [DOCUMENT NAME] describes

          [DOCUMENT ORGANIZATION DESCRIPTION]

^Bl.4 APPLICABLE DOCUMENTS^B

The following documents provide information necessary to
understanding this [DOCUMENT NAME].

          [LIST OF APPLICABLE DOCUMENTS]
```

Figure 2–7 Section 1 with WordStar Commands

You can further automate the Masters by creating templates and macros for information that is used globally.
Template files can be stored in separate template directories
or as part of document directories. These template files can
then be copied and edited according to the demands
of the document. For example, Figure 2–8 illustrates a roff
template for an end-user document preface.

```
\"January 1989 PREFACE TEMPLATE
.ce
.B
\s+2\f3PREFACE\s0
.sp .5i
.LP
.B
PURPOSE
.LP
This \f2[DOCUMENT NAME] Users Guide\fp provides
.sp .5i
.LP
\f3AUDIENCE\fp
.LP
The intended users of this guide are
.sp .5i
.LP
\f3ORGANIZATION\fp
.LP
This guide describes
.sp .5i
.LP
\f3DOCUMENTATION\fp
.LP
Related documentation includes:
.IP
.nf
\f2Compiler Library Users Guide
Micro Language Reference Guide
Micromecca S10/11 Users Guide
MicroSim Users Guide
S10/11 System Administrators Guide
MicroTime Users Guide\fp
.fi
```

Figure 2–8 Section 1 roff Template

Note that the preface template file contains a full alphabetic list of all product document titles. Entries in the list can then be edited out for documents to which they do not apply.

Macros can be constructed to call variables that are used globally, like the system identifier ([SYSTEM ID]) in development documents and the product name ([PRODUCT NAME]) in delivery documents.

You can automate the Masters even further by building a system in which full documents or sections containing all introductory material and current information can be called by menu selection. Packaged software is available to construct and design the menus.

3 Document Standards

Document standards are evidence of professionalism. The sooner the standards are incorporated in the documentation, the easier they are to learn and to enforce.

Technical writers employed during the project are generally assigned after specifications have been completed and often not until end-user documents have been drafted. Therefore:

> Software engineers who are not able to express themselves clearly in written communication should be enrolled in technical writing courses, and the skill should be required to be developed through training and experience. It is incorrect to assume that an employee who excels in the technical arena is not capable of improving his or her writing abilities, or that it is unimportant to do so. It must be stressed that documentation is the physical representation of the technical ideas and processes that lead to the implementation of the software system.[37]

Whoever is doing the writing needs standards to provide the consistency and structure vital to the production of successful technical publications.

It is imperative that these standards encompass all possible conditions that affect the preparation of different types of manuals. Once standards are developed, their application must be pursued on a continuing basis. This is essential for any documentation policy to be effective.[38]

The Document Masters have standards built in for consistency of format and introductory materials. These standards are based on structures very similar to those used in programming. The organizational techniques that have been touted in this hightech half of the century to write programs, such as structured programming, top-down design, and bottom-up definition, have been around for much longer as techniques to write scientific, pedantic, and entertaining essays.

Good writing is structured writing: consistency demands a top-down view of documentation in order that the system be described as an integrated whole, even though its parts are being defined, bottom-up, by different people.

TOP-DOWN

Discourse analysts often discuss the organization of reading comprehension in terms of "top-down effects."[39] Rather than processing letters in order to understand words, words in order to understand sentences, and so forth, readers process text top-down. That is, texts have meaning in terms of context. The parts derive meaning from the whole.

To achieve the top-down effect, text, like code, must be crafted as a logical, consistent pattern of syntax and presentation. The following standards apply to good writing, as well as to good programming.

Define constants. Constant terminology is not only a sure quality gauge of the final end-user publications, but a positive aid to internal communication.

Never trust a technical term until you are assured that a minimum of three people (preferably who have come from different companies) use the term to mean the same thing. Once everyone has agreed on a term, it should be used in all documentation about the system, from e-mail memos through publication release.

Assign variables to be logically consistent. Like all language structures, variables should show logical relationships based on parallelism (sets of like items). For example, establish parallel patterns for all groups of user commands and system messages listed in the documents so that, though each command varies, it is described in the same order, notation, and format.

Make appropriate logical connections. Just as an OR gate will not work where the correct decision rests on an AND, conjunctions have the power to make or break a logical connection in your reader's mind. For examples, *however* signals exception, and *therefore* proceeds a result. *But* and *thus* are their respective synonyms.

Show cause and effect only and always when it applies. Use *If . . . then* constructions, beginning with the *If* clause, to set up and fulfill the readers' expectations. For example, "If the power is decreased or the load is increased, then the backup power is automatically activated," or "If you choose option 3 on the Print Control Menu, then the following screen is displayed."

Provide obvious hooks. Transitions between paragraphs of text should have a logical basis, and each paragraph a consistent idea. Putting a temporary title above a paragraph is a good test for consistency.

Use strong verbs. Verbs are, of course, the very words on which a program is built, but they can function almost as strongly in written text. Avoid overuse of the verb *to be* (*is, are, was, were*); use active verbs instead. For example, "The system is capable of running 15 MIPS" could be made stronger— and shorter—changed to "The system can run at 15 MIPS."

Use punctuation precisely. Though punctuation is admittedly more critical in a program than in prose, the basic knowledge of punctuation is important to clear writing. Appendix A contains a robust subset of punctuation rules applicable to technical writing.

Use aliases for convenience. "ASIC" is quicker to write, and to read, than is "application specific integrated circuit." Use acronyms, rather than the spelled out term, after providing the spelled out term and acronym (in parenthesis) at the beginning of the document.

Some acronyms have gained the status of words; for example, *CPU* can stand for central processing unit, central processor unit, control processing unit, or control program unit, so don't use a spelled out term that would form a different acronym (for example, System Processing Unit).

Comment for easier reading. Introduce topics in the same order that you describe them. The Masters incorporate this technique whether the introduction is cast in sentence or in list format to help the reader skip from the known to the unknown more easily.

Avoid cross-references. Webs of cross-references in text don't work any better than tangled GOTOs, the major reason GOTOs have fallen from favor.

BOTTOM-UP

The fact of a common standard is much more important than the intrinsic character of the standard chosen.[40]

Just as important as creating and following standards for construction of all units of a system is creating and following standards for construction of all units of documentation. The following sections describe the units of end-user publications, grouped under front matter, back matter, and sections. You can use Appendix B to define the format for all the units in the final documents you will be turning out.

Front Matter

Front Matter standards include specifications for all the pages that precede the first section of the document. The front matter includes considerations for the following components.

Page numbering for front matter is generally lower case Roman.

Front cover stock and design depend on the way in which end-user documents are to be packaged; for example, slip-ins for binders, glossary stock, spiral binding, perfect binding.

The title page design can be stored as a template on which the title and version identification of the document can be changed.

Trademark notices protect your company's and other companies' trademarked and registered names. Figure 3–1 illustrates a sample trademark notice. The trademark notice can be stored as a template on which all trademarks are listed; entries can then be added as new products are developed or interfaced and edited out for documents in which the companies or products are not mentioned.

The following are trademarks of Micromecca Corporation and may only be used to define Micromecca Corporation products:

MICOMECCA 10/11 SUPER 10/11

VAX, MicroVAX, Ultrix, and **DEC** are trademarks of Digital Equipment Corporation. **UNIX** is a trademark of AT&T Bell Laboratories.

Figure 3–1 Sample Trademark Notice

The **copyright notice** establishes ownership of the document. Figure 3–2 illustrates a sample copyright notice. The copyright notice can be stored as a template on which publication dates can be added. The remainder of the template is boilerplate.

Copyright Micromecca Corporation 1988, 1989.

RESTRICTED RIGHTS LEGEND

Use, duplication, or disclosure by the Government is subject to restrictions as set forth in subparagraph (C) (1) (ii) of the Rights in Technical Data and Computer Software clause **252.227-7013.**

No part of this publication may be reproduced or translated, stored in a database or retrieval system, or transmitted in any form by electronic, mechanical, photocopying, recording, or other means, except as expressly permitted by Micromecca Corporation.

Figure 3–2 Sample Copyright Notice

If the document will contain command descriptions, then a boilerplate **notation table** can be included to provide the standard for writing and reading commands syntax. Figure 3–3 illustrates a sample notation table.

The **table of contents** standard includes the level which will list entries. Figure 3–4 illustrates a sample table of contents that includes four header levels.

Back Matter

Back Matter standards include specifications for all the pages that follow the last section of the document, including appendixes, a glossary, an index, and a back cover.

Appendixes need not be included in all technical publications, but they should be used to contain details that would break up the flow of information, for example, long tables, error messages, or lists of algorithms.

Multiple appendixes should be placed in the same order as they are first referred to in text.

Appendix format follows the rules according to content; for example, if you are presenting error messages, then use consistent error message format.

A **glossary** of terms should be included in every technical document. Technical terms vary from discipline to discipline and from company to company. Though a term may be defined when it is first used in text, readers don't necessarily read the document in sequence, nor should they have to search backward for the first mention of an uncommon acronym.

The glossary should include all acronyms defined by their spelled-out forms; all proper nouns in the publication defined in terms of physical and/or functional characteristics; all terms that you define or explain in the text. These terms vary greatly depending on the purpose and audience. You wouldn't want to gloss *read* in a reference guide, but might well do so in a guide meant for new data processing operators.

NOTATION	MEANING
command	Required in case shown (up/low)
KEYWORD	Required in case shown (up/low)
. , ( ) ; :	Required as shown
0 / \ $ #	Required as shown
" "	Contents required as shown
< · >	Required value of specified .type, where type is: c = a single character d = floating point or integer f = file pointer i = integer l = list s = string
[ ]	Optional
{ }	Choice
. . .	Repeat

EXAMPLES: SYNTAX NOTATION: sum <value.d> [<value.d>...]
COMMAND: sum 1 2 3

SYNTAX NOTATION: setflag <flagname.s> {TRUE FALSE}
COMMAND: setflag test TRUE

SYNTAX NOTATION: func <functionname.s> "{"<command.l>"}"
COMMAND: func doit { set x 12 }

NOTE: Any commands that do not conform to the above notation are noted in text.

Figure 3–3 Sample Notation Table

.

.

.

Figure 3–4　Sample Table of Contents

Use only the most common acronyms in the definition of any other term, for instance: *CPU* and *I/O*.

When referring to other glossary entries, include the reason for their relevance; for example, after the definition of *call*: "See *return* for called subroutine return options."

Alphabetize all glossary entries by the dictionary method rather than the telephone book method, that is, by letter rather than by word, as illustrated in Figure 3–5.

Data Bus Interface. The functional unit that controls other units' access to the Data Bus.

Data Code Table. The system table that controls user access to data. Only users with a code of 4 or above can access the table.

DB. Data Bus.

DBI. Data Bus Interface.

DCT. Data Control Table.

Figure 3–5 Glossary Organization

An **index** is an alphabetic list of significant subjects and the pages on which they are discussed in the publication.

Software publication indexes should provide both feature-oriented entries and task-oriented entries, as illustrated in Figure 3–6.

PRINT command, 21
Printing
    Graphics, 24
    Options, 21
    Program listings, 21
    Text files, 22 23

Figure 3–6 Index Subjects

Limit an index entry to three levels, beginning with the most general topic as the first-level entry, as illustrated in Figure 3–7.

```
database
   interface with system,  72,  73
   records,  43–47
    record fields,  48–63
   structure of,  2–5
```

Figure 3–7 Index Levels

Alphabetize entries at each level by the dictionary method rather than the telephone book method, that is, by letter rather than by word, as illustrated in Figure 3–8.

```
record format,  45
recording,  21
records,  43
sectors,  45
sector sharing,  46
```

Figure 3–8 Index Organization

A little trick of the trade to check the completeness of both your index and your text is to compare your index to a competitor's index. If the competitor has an index word or term you don't, check to see whether it is because you haven't included the word in the index or if your manual has left out that information.[41]

The **back cover** design, like the front cover design, depends on the way in which the end-user documents are to be packaged.

Sections

Document section, or chapter, standards include specifications for page layout, text divisions, figures, and tables.

Page numbering can be either sequential throughout the document or internal to each section. Numbering internally to each section makes it easier to update sections without having to renumber the whole document.

The **running head** and **running foot** on each page can be used to provide quick access to a particular section and to call out any limitation on the availability of the document, for example, "Proprietary Information."

A **header** consists of a number that places information at the correct sequential and hierarchical level in the text and a title that describes the information in that section. The format standard for headers in end-user documents might be specified as illustrated in Figure 3–9.

Header Specifications

1st level header centered, all caps, and bold; example:

1. INTRODUCTION

2nd level header flush left, all caps, and bold;
example:

1.1 I/O FUNCTIONS

3rd level header flush left, initial caps, and bold;
example:

1.1.1 Disk Access

4th level header flush left, initial caps, and
underlined; example:

1.1.1.1 Dedicated Disk

5th level header flush left, initial caps, period, and
bold; first sentence run in; example:

1.1.1.1.1 Physical ID. The following languages . . .

Figure 3–9 Header Format Specification

Paragraphs should be limited to a maximum number of sentences or lines. Ten lines maximum is a good rule of thumb to achieve more comprehensible, less intimidating text.

Warnings are generally used only if hardware is involved, to alert the reader to possible death or injury.

Cautions are used to call the readers' attention to possible equipment damage or program abort conditions.

Notes are used to notify the readers that an exception exists.

Examples should follow four important rules:[42]

1. Simple examples illustrate concepts; complex examples bury them.

2. Program output is important. If the program prints 17 pages of memory maps, it obviously is not necessary to include all of them. One or two partial pages, however, give the programmer some idea of what to expect during compilation or execution.

3. Program results are important. Sample programs should be realistic so computation results or printed reports can be included to show what actually happened.

4. Sample programs with errors are never going to execute. Run the program yourself to make sure it works. Always run it one last time from the final printed text to ensure against program code changes and typographical errors.

A **list** should be presented in parallel grammatic structure and consistent numbering notation, as the sample list in Figure 3–10 illustrates. The format standard for lists might be specified as illustrated in Figure 3–11.

A **figure** may be worth a thousand words, but it is rarely totally self-explanatory. Introduce a figure by its content, for example: "Figure 1–3 illustrates the calling structure." Figure 1–3 should then be titled "1–3. Calling Structure" and should illustrate descriptions in the text.

The following types of commands are available:

1. Line commands
    a. Text
        1) Paragraphs
        2) Tabs
    b. Graphics
        .
        .
        .

2. Menu commands
    a. Page control
        1) Font
            a) Point size
            b) Leading
        2) Spacing
        3) Running heads
        4) Running feet
    b. Text control
        .
        .
        .

    c. Graphics control
        .
        .
        .

    d. Output control

Figure 3–10 Sample List

If a figure needs symbols, acronyms, or abbreviations other than those used in text, then explain them in a key on the figure.

Figure titles are traditionally placed below the figure. If figures are members of a set, make their relationship clear in the title, for example:

**Figure 1–1. System Flow
(2 of 3)**

Avoid figures that make the readers turn the document sideways. Almost all figures can be set up to fit your page size or to run over multiple pages.

List Specifications

Introduction to list followed by a colon:

        1st level in list = 1., 2., . . .
        2nd level in list = a., b., . . .
        3rd level in list = 1), 2), . . .
        4th level in list = a), b), . . .

All entries in the list begin with a capital letter.
The other letters are generally all lowercase except
when an acronym or proper noun is used.

Figure 3–11 List Format Specification

The actual construction of figures depends on the resources available for professional and/or automated illustration.

Tables (matrices) are most efficiently used to help a reader locate a unique item of data at the intersection of logically related rows and columns. They can be used to effectively correlate tasks with resources, data with sources and destinations, and functions with modules.

Footnotes can be helpful in a table because of limited space. In software publications, indicate footnotes by a symbol other than an asterisk because asterisks are commonly used in program statements. In fact, it may be difficult to find a character on the keyboard that isn't used in some command syntax or other.

Table titles are traditionally placed above the table. If tables are continued over more than one page, then repeat the table title and column heads and provide a link, for example:

Table 1-4. SYSGEN Parameters (cont'd)

The format standard for a table might be specified as illustrated in Figure 3–12.

Table Specifications

1. Number the table with the chapter number, a hyphen, the table sequence number within the chapter, a period, and two spaces.

2. Set the word *Table* and all words in the title in initial caps.

3. Center the table title above each table.

4. Center column heads, full caps, over each column, and double underline.

5. Separate columns vertically with a single line.

6. Align words in columns by the first character.

7. Align numbers in columns by the decimal point.

8. Box the table.

Figure 3–12 Table Format Specification

Tables 3–1, 3–2, and 3–3 illustrate three sample instatiations of the table format standard.

Don't assume that, having made a table or a graph, *nothing* need be said about it. A little explanation of how to read the graph or table is often helpful. And almost invariably the significant relationships revealed by the table or graph should be pointed out.[43]

Table 3–1.   2-to-1 Multiplexer

S1	S0	A	B	F1	F2	Notes
0	0	X	X	0	1	disabled
0	1	0	X	0	1	
0	1	1	X	1	0	
1	0	X	0	0	1	
1	0	X	1	1	0	

X = don't care.

Table 3–2. Manufacturing Cost Accounting

MANUFACTURING	UNIT COST ($)	UNITS REQUIRED ($)	TOTAL UNIT COST ($)
Platform A			
Platform B			
TK50 tapes			
Reel tapes			
Personnel/hr.			
⋮			
		TOTAL COST:	$

Table 3–3. File Permissions

PERMISSIONS	OWNER	GROUP	OBJECT
-rwxrwxrwx	uucp	daemon	LOGFILE
-rwxrwxrwx	uucp	daemon	STST.sci
drwxrwxrwx	uucp	daemon	D.mini
drwxrwxrwx	uucp	daemon	D.mini
-rwxrwxrwx	uucp	daemon	ERRLOG
-rwxrwxrwx	uucp	daemon	SYSLOG
drwxrwxrwx	uucp	daemon	D.nodea0b1
drwxrwxrwx	uucp	daemon	D.a0b1
drwxr-xr-x	uucp	daemon	TM.
drwxr-xr-x	uucp	daemon	X.
drwxr-xr-x	uucp	daemon	D.
drwxr-xr-x	uucp	daemon	XTMP
drwxr-xr-x	uucp	daemon	C.

Spelling should be consistent to the letter, hyphenation, and capitalization. Your standards should include a spelling list to cover alternatives and approved terms.

Acronyms are discussed in Appendix C.

Abbreviations are discussed in Appendix C.

Symbols should conform to an existing standard, such as IEEE, or to the graphics system you are using.

4 Documentation Procedures

The content of each Document Master is based on the people who will be writing, reading, rewriting, and rereading the document throughout the product life-cycle. From this viewpoint, each document has end-users—the people who will be using it to get the information they need to proceed with their tasks; however, the discussions in this chapter use *end-user* in the standard industry way, to mean the person who uses the documentation along with the purchased product.

The procedures used to obtain, enter, validate, and produce information for your documents depend on your company rules and regimentations; however, the following basic flow of activities is entailed in producing all documents.

1. Plan and schedule documentation for the project and product.
2. Establish document control procedures, and track them along with the documents.
3. Generate the draft of information as fully as possible.
4. Have the draft reviewed by appropriate technical, managerial, and marketing personnel.
5. Update the previous draft by adding new information and highlighting new questions and remaining or additional missing information in the text.

6. Have the final draft signed off by the designated title holder.

7. Produce and distribute the end-user manuals, including copy editing, formatting, producing the print master text and graphics; reproducing the number of copies needed adding front matter and back matter, and binding the documents to be delivered with the system.

Steps 1 and 2 involve subject experts, managers, and administrators responsible for planning and tracking phases of the project.

Steps 3 through 5 are repetitive, like most activities in the design phases, and involve managers, technologists, the document controller, and usually technical writers by the second or third iteration. The developer corrects and adds information to the review draft and, optionally, delivers it to a technical writer. If a developer hates to write, he or she should have the help of a technical writer. Writing expertise will help the people who have to read the document, too.

Step 6 involves the people who have final responsibility for the document's content. In the case of end-user documents, technical, marketing, and legal signoff may be necessary. The developer and/or writer and document controller resolve any anomalies until the draft is signed off.

Step 7 involves editors and production staff and/or vendor services in addition to the responsible writer.

Obviously both leadership and teamwork are vital to the success of the documentation process.

The final measures of success are:[44]

- Collectively achieved productivity.
- Creativity and innovation elicited through both doing things right and doing wrong things.
- Satisfaction for team members.

The following sections briefly describe the documentation processes in terms of:

- Scheduling documentation
- Establishing document control
- Generating drafts
- Getting and giving reviews
- Producing end-user publications

SCHEDULING DOCUMENTATION

Documentation scheduling—especially for end-user documents—should start with the project.

> An understanding of the problems of documentation production, publication, and maintenance levies a requirement for early planning of this area of the project in great detail. The problems are not only those concerned with composing written communication reflecting technical excellence but also those concerned with the mechanics of publishing a document. An understanding of the complicated and interdependent set of factors affecting documentation production even levies a requirement for additional documents—formatting guides, style guides, and documentation production procedures. It has implications that touch the scheduling, organization, staffing requirements, and cost of the project and that must be addressed at the very beginning in order to avert major project problems.[45]

Figure 4–1 illustrates a high-level view of the project workflow and the documentation milestones in that workflow. A workflow diagram is useful not only for scheduling and tracking, but also for establishing relationships and history to aid in scheduling documents on succeeding projects.

All steps in the documentation process should be accommodated in the Project Master Schedule and in the schedules

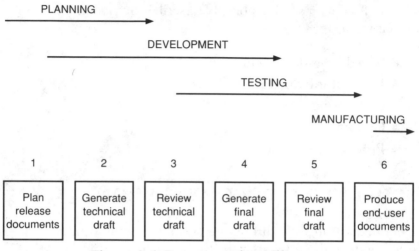

Figure 4–1 Documentation Milestones

of each organization that will be involved. For example, the draft reviewers should be identified as early as possible so that they can build some time into their schedules.

In order to schedule the documents into the Project Master Schedule, you can use the following approximate percentages of the total time spent on each documentation milestone:

1. Plan release documentation   2%
2. Generate technical draft   30%
3. Review technical draft   20%
4. Generate final draft   20%
5. Review final draft   3%
6. Produce end-user documents   <u>25%</u>
                       100%

NOTE that milestones 2 and 3 can be decomposed and reiterated as many times as is feasible in the project schedule. In general, the more iterations, the better the documents.

To calculate the time needed for each document:

1. Estimate the page count of the document.
2. Multiply the page count by 4 hours for an update OR 5 hours for a new document. **NOTE** that no explicit fudge factor is included; the multiplier of 4 hours for update publications and 5 hours for new publications covers the length (and breadth) of the project. In most large projects it is the barebones minimum time required, barely taking time for vacations, replacements, illness, management, meetings, and so forth into account.
3. Divide by 40 hours per week. Use weeks rather than days to calculate documentation time for large projects, as calculating to a finer grain is more time consuming and generally not more accurate.

Figure 4–2 illustrates an example calculation for the time needed in the schedule for one new users guide.

[PRODUCT NAME] Users Guide

    200 pages estimate

    × 5 (new document)

    1000 hours

1. Plan release document	2%	2 hours	(of total release 3.1)
2. Generate technical draft	30%	300 hours	
3. Review technical draft	20%	200 hours	
4. Generate final draft	20%	200 hours	
5. Review final draft	3%	3 hours	
6. Produce end-user document	25%	250 hours	

       955 hrs ÷ 40 = 23.6 weeks

Figure 4–2 New Publication Schedule

RELEASE: 3.1

RELEASE DATE: 9/4/89

PUBLICATIONS	ESTIMATED PAGES	WEEKS
MicroBlock Users Manual	20 new	2.5
MicroModule Users Manual	85 new	10.5
MicroChip Users Manual	80 new	10.0
MicroSim Users Manual	100 new	12.5
MicroTime Users Manual	100 new	12.5
MicroGenesis Users Manual	200 update	20.0
Release Description	25 new	3.0
Update Package	10 update	1.0

72.0 weeks

÷ 3 = 24 weeks

Figure 4–3 Publication Release Plan

To calculate the total number of weeks needed for documentation:

1. Total the weeks needed for each document.
2. Divide by the number of developer/writer/production staff available for documentation.

Figure 4–3 illustrates an example calculation for the time needed in the schedule for a release of end-user documents.

NOTE that the total time needed is calculated in real time—not elapsed time.

As first customer ship (FCS) approaches, the pace becomes more frantic and fraught with occurrences of Murphy's Law. If the publication plan becomes the critical path in the Project Master Schedule, then the following strategies can be employed:

1. Hire adequate staff and/or
2. Compress the workflow by skipping iterations of draft generation and review and/or
3. Include some update information in the *Release Description*, and update the appropriate manual after release.

To calculate the quality of documentation, consider the real total time available, the time actually devoted to each documentation milestone, the writing and reviewing skills of the developers, the experience of the technical writers, and the resources available for inputting, editing, and production.

Both quantity and quality dictate that documentation scheduling be noted and updated continually so that the resources of time, personnel, and equipment can be dynamically adjusted in view of FCS and that the quality of all the documentation—and of the jobs—does not suffer.

ESTABLISHING DOCUMENT CONTROL

The problem is not to restrict information, but to ensure that relevant information gets to all the people who need it.[46]

In order for information to be relevant, document control must be established to protect the integrity of the documents. The better the internal control of the documents, the better their chance for containing current accurate information throughout the project. The better the external control, the better the chance that the information gets to all the people who need it.

Document control can be put under the umbrella of system configuration management. However, the most efficient way to control all project documents is to locate the data in a centralized site and place its maintenance under the control of a designated document controller.

For the specification and development documents that contain sensitive or classified information, additional internal and external controls will have to be put in place.

Internal Controls

Internal document control procedures should be set up to store and protect online and hardcopy versions of all documents.

Online

The document controller should be responsible for the organization and location of documentation computer files.

In a hierarchical **directory** system, each computer file can be easily mapped to the Project Masters Directory illustrated in Figure 2–5.

The **filename** can be constructed of the acronym for the document followed by a dot and the version identifier, for example, srs.1. Using numbers rather than letters for version identifiers is less confusing when using acronyms for filenames. Figure 4–4 illustrates a filesystem of Document Masters that conforms to this convention.

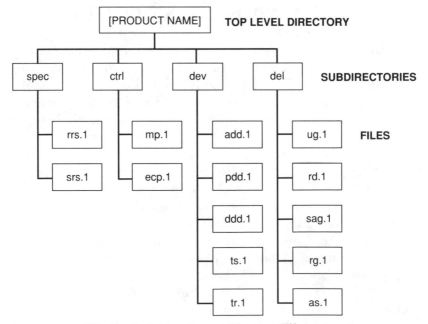

Figure 4–4 Document Masters Filesystem

As each new **revision** of the file is begun, change the version identifier (for example, srs.1 to srs.2). If you wish to keep previous versions of the document online, then you can copy the previous version into a separate archive directory before updating the version identifier and the contents of the file.

Files should be accorded **read/write privileges** based on the sensitivity of the information and the document development environment. When the environment allows file sharing, controls will need to be more stringent than when the environment is an independent work station.

File **backup** is critical protection. If files are to be backed up according to a company schedule, then be aware of that schedule. If files are to be stored on floppy disks, then a backup disk or two should be made in the event of damage to a disk or files. The backup should be marked with the names of the files and the date and time of backup. If currency checking is available in your system, then you can trust it to give you the dates and times; however, filenames and dates on the floppy are a double check in case of hardware failures.

Hardcopy

For document control of hardcopy, the document controller should establish notation for the original version identifier (whether it is blank, -0, -1, or $-A$) and the conditions under which the identifier is incremented.

All documents should share a common cover sheet that identifies the document, the current version, and the individual finally responsible for the document content. As the document proceeds through the life-cycle phases, the responsible individual may change. The change must be reflected on the cover sheet. Figure 4–5 illustrates a cover sheet template.

[DOCUMENT NAME]

FOR

[PRODUCT/SYSTEM ID]

[VERSION NUMBER]

Responsible Individual:

NAME: [RESPONSIBLE INDIVIDUAL NAME]

TITLE: [RESPONSIBLE INDIVIDUAL TITLE]

Figure 4–5 Cover Sheet Template

To track hardcopy, you can make a master list of the documents under control and indicate the status of each as it progresses through the project phases and the documentation processes. Figure 4–6 illustrates a Documentation Status Form. Of course, the Documentation Status Form can be kept online for easy updating.

Hardcopy documents should be filed alphabetically. You can archive all documents in a previous version in one location or file all versions of one document together, from oldest (in back) to newest.

External Controls

External document control procedures should be set up to cover submission, distribution, and retrieval of documents throughout the project.

DOCUMENT NAME	VERSION NUMBER					CURRENT RESPONSIBILITY
	-1	-2	-3	-4	-5	
System Requirements Specification	X	X	X	X		Pat Jones for text processing
Resource Requirements Specification	X	X	X			Chris Smith for review
Management Plan	X	X				Sandy Brown for updating
Engineering Change Proposal						Lee Green
Architecture Design Document						
Prototype Design Document						
Detailed Design Document						
Test Specifications						
Test Reports						
Users Guide						
Release Description						
Reference Guide						
System Administrators Guide						
Acceptance Signoff						

Figure 4–6 Documentation Status Form

Submission

The procedures for submitting a new document to document control should establish the following:

1. The method to submit a document to the control system.
2. Security levels and their implementation.
3. The approval necessary in order for a document to be accepted.
4. The physical form of the document (online file, floppy, hardcopy).
5. The person finally responsible for the document.

Distribution

The procedures for distributing document copies from document control should establish the following:

1. The method to add a name to a distribution list.
2. Security levels and their implementation.
3. The approval necessary in order for a name to be accepted.
4. The physical form of the document.
   a. If the document is online, then how to grant access and read/write privileges.
   b. If the document is hardcopy, then how to add the requester's name to the distribution list.

The most critical distribution in the life-cycle is review copies. A Review Approval Form should be attached to each review draft. The form should include:

1. The names of responsible distributor and receiver.
2. Indication of the status of the review in the cycle.
3. Fields for approval status.
4. Dates of distribution, expected return, and real return.

Figure 4–7 illustrates a sample Review Approval Form template.

To: [DISTRIBUTION LIST]

From:

Date:

Subject: Document-in-Process

[DOCUMENT NAME] [VERSION NUMBER] _____ is in
the following stage:

_____ technical review

_____ final review

_____ update / revision

Please review the attached copy, check your approval
preference, sign, and return by __/__/__.

_____ I approve; continue to next phase.

_____ I approve upon incorporation of the specified changes.

_____ I withhold approval until resolution of major changes.

Name: _____

Title: _____

Date: __/__/__

Figure 4–7 Review Approval Form Template

Retrieval

Timely retrieval and resolution of outstanding documents is an important document control function. When a document draft has not been returned in the specified time, it should be the document controller's responsibility to track it down, often under a pile of program listings or engineering drawings.

For the end-user documents that need legal authorization, generally systems with hardware components that are potentially dangerous, be sure that you have the authorization before going any further.

GENERATING DRAFTS

Generating drafts involves both cooperative interviewing skills and solitary writing skills.

Interviews

A good draft is often the result of effective communication. If you are a technical writer, a manager, or a developer who is responsible for writing a draft in any phase of the project, then you will be seeking information from others. Formal and informal interviews are the medium of communication, and the method should be a combination of old-fashioned consideration and hightech equipment.[47]

Schedule time. After having established a rapport with the interviewee, calling or dropping in to ask a pertinent question is efficient and usually welcome. But at the beginning, set up official times.

Prepare a list of questions focused on an overview of the subject before getting to the details. Have plenty of paper and different colored pens for explanations by diagram, which seems to come naturally to all segments of the hightech community. It is much easier to carry a sketch back to your desk than to try to copy information off a whiteboard while the members of the next meeting file in.

Use a tape recorder for long sessions. The tape recorder allows you to look at the speaker rather than to be scribbling answers; keeps you and your interviewee on track, less likely to wander from the subject; and records spontaneous questions in cases where the explanations are unexpected, incomplete, or incomprehensible.

If transcribing the tapes is too time consuming for the payback in text, you can still listen, take notes, and write the information into the draft. Even if you asked all the right questions at the interview, you probably won't recall all the right answers.

Writing

Organizing and writing the information in the draft requires writing skills. Whether you hold the title of technical writer or not, when you are providing written descriptions of technical systems, then you are tech writing.

Just as an engineer must understand material properties; a systems programmer, console modes; a field service rep, diagnostic functions; and a marketeer, the market, so must a competent writer understand rhetorical devices in order to achieve the most elegant and proper solutions. Understanding grammar, its usage and structure, is basic to all good writing.

In addition to your company documentation standards, any one of a half dozen college handbooks, Strunk and White's *Elements of Style*, a copy of *The Chicago Manual of Style*, and a dictionary—all in easy reach—are requisites on a writer's desk.

GETTING & GIVING REVIEWS

Good reviews are perhaps the most important part of good documentation. Good reviews are not "hey there, great job," but are the result of careful reading, meticulous editing, and timely return of documents. Good reviews are hard to come by.

> Often reviewers just read through a document, changing grammar, spelling, and punctuation. Rarely do they look at the document's organization. Although they often note inconsistencies or inaccuracies in the material before them, only rarely do they notice that material is missing. And a manual that is missing important information fails in the areas of completeness and usefulness.[48]

At all companies, the politics can get especially heated during final review when publication drafts must be critiqued by developers, marketeers, customer service personnel, quality controllers, and lawyers, all of whom won't agree with parts of the publication—or with each other—and few of whom will acknowledge limits to their critical ability.

If you receive a document with Review Approval Form withholding approval, then call immediately to begin resolution of the problem.

If you receive conflicting comments, resolve the inconsistencies by meeting with the disagreeing reviewers. A strategy must be devised to mediate among:[49]

- Technologists who return copies untouched, late, or not at all;

- Sales people who sometimes learn from the review draft that features they were touting to prospective customers didn't make it into the product;

- Managers who have published articles and decide the tone of the manual is somehow wrong; and

- The company lawyer, who has just found that the product name has already been registered by another company in the same industry.

Thomas Barker offers a survey of strategies to combat lacking feedback[50], but the major strategy is NO SURPRISES.

There is always time to give everyone responsible for signing off the final review draft a preliminary view of its contents, its prototype.

When the draft appears as clean as it went out (except for a typo or two that the reviewer has spotted), the reason is most likely not a perfect document, but a reviewer whose manager has not made it clear that the documentation is important by providing the perqs to prove it.

PRODUCING END-USER PUBLICATIONS

The documents that are delivered with the product are the culmination of the documentation effort. They are an indication and reflection of the product.

A user manual serves three important functions:[51]

- It provides practical information when formal classroom instruction is not available.

- It helps the inexperienced to get started quickly.

- It helps the experienced to become productive quickly.

The perspective of the document end-users shifts dramatically from needing to know how the system works to needing to know how to make the system work, both initially and over time. The following sections briefly describe the end-users and their needs for documents and revisions.

End-Users

Any or all of the following groups may be end-users of a single product and the audience for the documents that accompany it:

Professional users who need to understand the system in terms of their use for it, for instance, accounting, mechanical design, medical or geological research.

Nontechnical users who need easy to follow instructions in order to use the functions provided by the system.

Application programmers who need to know how to create, modify, or troubleshoot their application in the system.

Systems programmers who need complete descriptions of operating system functions and implications presented in consistent patterns.

System administrators who need to know what is required and what to expect from each available operation.

Documents

To make all your end-user documents fit the needs and expectations of their audiences:

Organize the information as well as possible. If you use the Masters with little modification, then continue to observe the rules of good organization within each section, especially the structures of parallelism and hierarchies, and the document standards.

Ditto even if you choose to modify the Masters.

Make the manuals as short as possible. Various methods of condensation are available to "make the haystack smaller":[52]

1. Summarize in a concise handbook, or a reference card, or a poster.

2. Customize so that a complex product is described by the task at hand. Only if you expect the same end-user to install, service, and use its capabilities does all the information need to be in one physical document.

3. Cull and winnow unnecessary information. As it does for many applications, the 80–20 Rule generally

works for documentation: 80% of the work can be done with 20% of the documentation. The trick is to be sure the 20% is easily accessible and the other 80% is available to the few with a need to know.

Involve the reader with the product as soon as possible. Most of your audience is reading a manual as the necessary evil preceding the good they expect the product is going to bring them, so get to the good part.

The end-user needs the documentation to learn the application. Learners notoriously don't bother with overviews and previews. They want to use the system now. If the manual supports a computer product, then tell the readers how to logon right away—and how to logoff right after that. If it's a maintenance manual, then lead the reader through the procedures necessary to fix the problem, right now.

One solution is a "Minimal Manual," bare bones, eliminating all repetition, summaries, reviews; organizing chapters in less than three pages, including specific error recovery information for typical errors; making chapter headings task oriented so that the table of contents could also serve for an index.[53]

Though the minimal manual is a noble experiment, it will work only if the rest of the information is available when the reader is ready to do more than just bare bones work.

Present as professional a publication as possible with the allotted resources. Preparing the final copy of text is the last chance to catch errors.

The last five percent of the work makes the document 100 percent better.[54] And editing is the key.

Editors can make substantial contributions to their company's image and product quality. But editors must have management's support in the form of policies and procedures that will give the editing function professional legitimacy and authority. Editors, then, are compelled to exercise this authority sensibly and accurately, thereby proving through example the legitimacy of their function.[55]

Becoming a good editor requires discipline and continual practice. Luckily, while you're practicing, you're getting it done.

When you begin to edit, remember, there's only so much time (never enough). The accuracy and organization of the information comes first, so read predominately for technical content first and grammar and mechanics second.

No amount of editing on screen is sufficient for a document that will be delivered on paper. The final edit and the print copy that will be used to reproduce the document should be edited on hardcopy, especially for format standards.

Use typestyles, white space, figures, and tables to arrange each page both logically and aesthetically.

Check the print master one more time, slowly, before delivering it for reproducing or typesetting.

Revisions

Large projects generally produce single or multiple products that are expected to be updated and enhanced over several years. Each release of the product requires a *Release Description* and eventually revision of the documents that describe it.

The pages in the existing document that contain any additions or deletions made to text, figures, tables, and appendixes should be marked with a change bar at the beginning of each line that contains changed material. Change bars help readers already familiar with the material to see what has changed and to help new readers to track the product evolution. Because change bars are meant to call attention to the latest changes, remove any bars from previous revisions before adding new ones for new revisions.

After determining how the content changes have affected the physical form of the end-user publication, help the user update existing manuals by providing instructions.

Figure 4–8 illustrates sample revision instructions.

September 1989

Dear Micromecca User:

The enclosed pages replace pages of your
current **Micromecca Block Library Users Guide.**

All replacement pages are dated "Sep 1989." Changes
are indicated by change bars in the outside margin.

The following list of replacement pages is included
for your convenience:

Volume I :	Title Page	
	Table of Contents	
	Chapter 5	5-39 / 5-40
		5-43 / 5-44
		5-65 / 5-66
	Chapter 7	7-5 / 7-6
	Chapter 8	all
Volume II :	Title Page	
	Table of Contents	
	Chapter 1	all
	Chapter 4	4-1 / 4-2
		4-3 / 4-4
	Chapter 11	all

Figure 4–8 Sample Revision Instructions

PART II

SPECIFYING THE SYSTEM

Masters for specifying the system include:

SYSTEM REQUIREMENTS SPECIFICATION
RESOURCE REQUIREMENTS SPECIFICATION

5 System Requirements Specification

4.5.3 System Capacities
    4.5.3.1 Internal Storage Requirements
    4.5.3.2 Execution Time Requirements
    4.5.3.3 Interface Bandwidths
4.6 Maintainability
4.7 Testability
4.8 Flexibility
4.9 Portability
4.10 Interoperability
(4.n [ADDITIONAL PERFORMANCE REQUIREMENT])

5. INTERFACE REQUIREMENTS

5.1 [SYSTEM ID]-to-User Interface Requirements
    5.1.1 Displays
    5.1.2 Controls
    5.1.3 Diagnostics
5.2 [SYSTEM ID]-to-Software Interface Requirements
5.3 [SYSTEM ID]-to-Hardware Interface Requirements

6. VERIFICATION REQUIREMENTS

6.1 General Test Requirements
6.2 Special Test Requirements

([APPENDIX])

GLOSSARY

1. SCOPE

The following subsections describe the scope of this [SYSTEM ID] System Requirements Specification (SRS) in terms of its purpose, audience, organization, and applicable documents.

1.1 Purpose

This SRS specifies requirements for a [SYSTEM FUNCTION(S)] system.

1.2 Audience

The intended users of this SRS are [USER TITLES] (with [PRE-REQUISITE KNOWLEDGE]).

1.3 Organization

This SRS describes the [SYSTEM ID] system requirements in terms of:
   [DOCUMENT ORGANIZATION DESCRIPTION]

1.4 Applicable Documents

The following documents provide information necessary to understanding this SRS.
   [LIST OF APPLICABLE DOCUMENTS]

2. EXECUTIVE SUMMARY

The following subsections summarize the [SYSTEM ID] System functional, performance, and interface requirements.

2.1 Functions

The [SYSTEM ID] System will provide the following major functions.
   [LIST OF MAJOR FUNCTIONS]

2.2 Performance

The [SYSTEM ID] System must meet the following performance criteria.
[LIST OF PERFORMANCE CRITERIA]

2.3 Interfaces

The [SYSTEM ID] System will interface with the following end-users, software, and hardware.
[LIST OF INTERFACES]

3. FUNCTIONAL REQUIREMENTS

The following subsections specify and describe each functional requirement.

3.n [FUNCTION NAME]

The following subsections describe [FUNCTION NAME] in terms of purpose, inputs, and outputs.

3.n.1 Purpose

[FUNCTION NAME] serves the following purpose:
[PURPOSE OF FUNCTION]

3.n.2 Inputs

The following table lists all inputs to [FUNCTION NAME] and describes them in terms of purpose, source(s), legality checks, and error indication and recovery.
Table n. [FUNCTION NAME] Input Table
[INPUT TABLE]

3.n.3 Outputs

The following table lists all outputs to be generated by [FUNCTION NAME] and describes them in terms of purpose, destination(s), legality checks, and error indication and recovery.

Table n. [FUNCTION NAME] Output Table
[OUTPUT TABLE]

4. PERFORMANCE REQUIREMENTS

The following subsections specify the performance requirements applicable to [SYSTEM ID] in terms of:

1. Correctness
2. Reliability
3. Efficiency
4. Integrity
5. Adaptability
6. Maintainability
7. Testability
8. Flexibility
9. Portability
10. Reusability
11. Interoperability
(n. [ADDITIONAL PERFORMANCE REQUIREMENT])

Each requirement is stated as a degree or range in which the requirement must apply.

4.1 Correctness

The system will satisfy the requirements specified in this SRS to the following degree of correctness.
[CORRECTNESS REQUIREMENT]

4.2 Reliability

The system will consistently perform its intended function to the following degree of reliability.
[RELIABILITY REQUIREMENT]

4.3 Efficiency

The system will use computer resources to the following degree of efficiency.

4.3.n [RESOURCE NAME]
[EFFICIENCY REQUIREMENT]

4.4 Integrity

The system will control unauthorized access to operations and data to the following degree of integrity.
[INTEGRITY REQUIREMENTS]

4.5 Adaptability

The following subsections describe adaptability requirements in terms of:

1. System environment
2. System parameter
3. System capacities

4.5.1 System Environment

The following lists the environmental ranges in which installations can operate the system.
[LIST OF SYSTEM ENVIRONMENTAL REQUIREMENTS]

4.5.2 System Parameters

The following parameters can be changed within their specified ranges according to operational needs.
[LIST OF PARAMETERS & RANGES]

4.5.3 System Capacities

The following describes storage and workload capacities that are to be redefinable according to operational needs.

4.5.3.1 Internal Storage Requirements
[INTERNAL STORAGE SIZE]

4.5.3.2 Execution Time Requirements
[EXECUTION TIME LIMITS]

4.5.3.3 Interface Bandwidths
[LIST OF INTERFACE NAMES AND BANDWIDTHS]

4.6 Maintainability

The system will be maintainable to the following maximum effort required to locate and fix an error.
[MAXIMUM EFFORT TO LOCATE AN ERROR]
[MAXIMUM EFFORT TO FIX AN ERROR]

4.7 Testability

The system will be testable to the following maximum effort required to ensure its intended functions.
[LIST OF TESTABILITY REQUIREMENTS]

4.8 Flexibility

The system will be flexible to the following maximum effort required for enhancements.
[LIST OF FLEXIBILITY REQUIREMENTS]

4.9 Portability

The system will be portable to the following maximum effort required to transfer from one hardware or software environment to another.
[LIST OF PORTABILITY REQUIREMENTS]

4.10 Interoperability

The system will facilitate interfacing with other systems to the following degrees.
[LIST OF INTEROPERABILITY REQUIREMENTS]

(4.n [ADDITIONAL PERFORMANCE REQUIREMENT]

The system will [ADDITIONAL PERFORMANCE REQUIRE-MENT].
[REQUIREMENT SPECIFICATION])

5. INTERFACE REQUIREMENTS

The following Interface Block Diagram illustrates the [SYSTEM ID] interfaces to end-users, software, and hardware.
[INTERFACE BLOCK DIAGRAM]
Figure n. [SYSTEM ID] Interface Block Diagram
The following subsections describe interface requirements in terms of end-users, software, and hardware.

5.1 [SYSTEM ID]-to-User Interface Requirements

The following subsections describe the [SYSTEM ID] user interface requirements in terms of:

1. Displays.
2. Controls.
3. Diagnostics.

5.1.1 Displays

The following display types will be available.
[LIST OF DISPLAY TYPES]

5.1.2 Controls

The following operator controls will be available.
[LIST OF OPERATOR CONTROLS]

5.1.3 Diagnostics

The following describes utilities that will be available for system diagnostics.
[LIST OF DIAGNOSTIC UTILITIES]

5.2 [SYSTEM ID]-to-Software Interface Requirements

The following [SYSTEM ID]-to-Software Interface Summary Table describes the interfacing software requirements in terms of:

1. Information
2. Control
3. Data
4. Message

Table n. Software Interface Summary Table
[SOFTWARE INTERFACE SUMMARY TABLE]

5.3 [SYSTEM ID]-to-Hardware Interface Requirements

The following [SYSTEM ID]-to-Hardware Interface Summary Table describes the interfacing hardware requirements in terms of:

1. Information
2. Control
3. Data
4. Message

Table n. Hardware Interface Summary Table
[HARDWARE INTERFACE SUMMARY TABLE]

6. VERIFICATION REQUIREMENTS

The following subsections describe the general and special test methods, techniques, and tools that will be used to verify that the system satisfies its requirements.

6.1 General Test Requirements

The following test methods will be used to verify that the system requirements have been satisfied.

1. Demonstration. Observable functional operation of the system (or some part of the system) not requiring the use of special instrumentation or test equipment.

2. Data Recording and Analysis. Operation of the system (or some part of the system) and collection and subsequent observations, interpretations, and extrapolations made from the data.

(n. [ADDITIONAL TEST METHOD].
    [ADDITIONAL TEST METHOD DESCRIPTION])

6.2 Special Test Requirements

The following special tools, techniques, facilities, and acceptance limits will be employed to verify the system requirements.
    [LIST OF SPECIAL TEST REQUIREMENTS
        AND DESCRIPTION OF EACH]

([APPENDIX TITLE]

The following information details [SUBJECT OF APPENDIX].
    [TEXT OF APPENDIX])

GLOSSARY

The following terms and acronyms are used throughout [SYSTEM ID] documentation.
    [LIST OF TERMS AND ACRONYMS
        AND THEIR DEFINITIONS]

6 Resource Requirements Specification

1. **SCOPE**

   1.1 Purpose
   1.2 Audience
   1.3 Organization
   1.4 Applicable Documents

2. **EXECUTIVE SUMMARY**

   2.1 Development Resources
   2.2 Testing Resources
   2.3 Customer Services Resources
   2.4 Delivery Resources

3. **DEVELOPMENT RESOURCE REQUIREMENTS**

   3.1 Development Personnel
   3.2 Development Equipment
   3.3 Development Software
   3.4 Development Facilities
   3.5 Development Schedule

4. **TESTING RESOURCE REQUIREMENTS**

   4.1 Testing Personnel
   4.2 Testing Equipment
   4.3 Testing Software
   4.4 Testing Facilities
   4.5 Testing Schedule

5. CUSTOMER SERVICES RESOURCE REQUIREMENTS

5.1 Documentation Resources
    5.1.1 Documentation Personnel
    5.1.2 Documentation Equipment
    5.1.3 Documentation Software
    5.1.4 Documentation Facilities
    5.1.5 Documentation Schedule
5.2 Training Resources
    5.2.1 Training Personnel
    5.2.2 Training Equipment
    5.2.3 Training Software
    5.2.4 Training Facilities
    5.2.5 Training Schedule
5.3 Customer Support Resources
    5.3.1 Customer Support Personnel
    5.3.2 Customer Support Equipment
    5.3.3 Customer Support Software
    5.3.4 Customer Support Facilities
    5.3.5 Customer Support Schedule

6. DELIVERY RESOURCE REQUIREMENTS

6.1 Manufacturing Resources
    6.1.1 Manufacturing Personnel
    6.1.2 Manufacturing Equipment
    6.1.3 Manufacturing Software
    6.1.4 Manufacturing Facilities
    6.1.5 Manufacturing Schedule
6.2 Distribution Resources
    6.2.1 Distribution Personnel
    6.2.2 Distribution Equipment
    6.2.3 Distribution Software
    6.2.4 Distribution Facilities
    6.2.5 Distribution Schedule

([APPENDIX])

GLOSSARY

1. SCOPE

The following subsections describe the scope of this [SYSTEM ID] Resource Requirement Specification (RRS) in terms of its purpose, audience, organization, and applicable documents.

1.1 Purpose

This RRS specifies resources necessary to support the [SYSTEM ID] System throughout its life-cycle.

1.2 Audience

The intended users of this RRS are [USER TITLES] (with [PRE-REQUISITE KNOWLEDGE]).

1.3 Organization

This RRS describes the [SYSTEM ID] resource requirements in terms of:
　　　[DOCUMENT ORGANIZATION DESCRIPTION]

1.4 Applicable Documents

The following documents provide information necessary to understanding this RRS.
　　　[SYSTEM ID] System Requirements Specification
　　　([LIST OF OTHER APPLICABLE DOCUMENTS])

2. EXECUTIVE SUMMARY

The following subsections summarize the resources required to support the [SYSTEM ID] System development, testing, customer services, and delivery.

2.1 Development Resources

The following are the totals for the resources required for system development.

Personnel:

[DEVELOPMENT PERSONNEL TOTAL]

Equipment:

[DEVELOPMENT EQUIPMENT TOTAL]

Software:

[DEVELOPMENT SOFTWARE TOTAL]

2.2 Testing Resources

The following are the totals for the resources required for system verification.

Personnel:

[TESTING PERSONNEL TOTAL]

Equipment:

[TESTING EQUIPMENT TOTAL]

Software:

[TESTING SOFTWARE TOTAL]

2.3 Customer Services Resources

The following are the totals for the resources required for customer services.

Personnel:

[CUSTOMER SERVICES PERSONNEL TOTAL]

Equipment:

[CUSTOMER SERVICES EQUIPMENT TOTAL]

Software:
> [CUSTOMER SERVICES SOFTWARE TOTAL]

2.4 Delivery Resources

The following are the total for the resources required for system delivery.

Personnel:
> [DELIVERY PERSONNEL TOTAL]

Equipment:
> [DELIVERY EQUIPMENT TOTAL]

Software:
> [DELIVERY SOFTWARE TOTAL]

3. DEVELOPMENT RESOURCE REQUIREMENTS

The following subsections describe resources required for system development in terms of personnel, equipment, software, facilities, and schedule.

3.1 Development Personnel

The following types and number of personnel are required for development.
> [LIST OF DEVELOPMENT PERSONNEL TYPES
> AND NUMBER REQUIRED]

3.2 Development Equipment

The following equipment is required for development.
> [LIST OF DEVELOPMENT EQUIPMENT
> AND BRIEF DESCRIPTION OF EACH]

3.3 Development Software

The following software is required for development.

[LIST OF DEVELOPMENT SOFTWARE
AND BRIEF DESCRIPTION OF EACH]

3.4 Development Facilities

The following facilities are required for development.
[LIST OF DEVELOPMENT FACILITIES
AND BRIEF DESCRIPTION OF EACH]

3.5 Development Schedule

The following milestones are required for development.
[LIST OF DEVELOPMENT MILESTONES
AND BRIEF DESCRIPTION OF EACH]
[DEVELOPMENT MILESTONE CHART]
Figure n. Development Schedule

4. TESTING RESOURCE REQUIREMENTS

The following subsections describe resources required for system testing in terms of personnel, equipment, software, facilities, and schedule.

4.1 Testing Personnel

The following types and number of personnel are required for testing.
[LIST OF PERSONNEL TYPES AND NUMBER REQUIRED]

4.2 Testing Equipment

The following equipment is required for testing.
[LIST OF TESTING EQUIPMENT
AND BRIEF DESCRIPTION OF EACH]

4.3 Testing Software

The following software is required for testing.
[LIST OF TESTING SOFTWARE
AND BRIEF DESCRIPTION OF EACH]

4.4 Testing Facilities

The following facilities are required for testing.
[LIST OF TESTING FACILITIES
AND BRIEF DESCRIPTION OF EACH]

4.5 Testing Schedule

The following milestones are required for testing.
[LIST OF TESTING MILESTONES
AND BRIEF DESCRIPTION OF EACH]
[TESTING MILESTONE CHART]
Figure n. Testing Schedule

5. CUSTOMER SERVICES RESOURCE REQUIREMENTS

The following subsections describe resources required for customer services in terms of documentation, training, and customer support.

5.1 Documentation Resources

The following subsection describes resources required for documentation development and production in terms of personnel, equipment, software, facilities, and schedule.

5.1.1 Documentation Personnel

The following types and number of personnel are required for documentation.
[LIST OF DOCUMENTATION PERSONNEL TYPES
AND NUMBER REQUIRED]

5.1.2 Documentation Equipment

The following equipment is required for documentation.
[LIST OF DOCUMENTATION EQUIPMENT
AND BRIEF DESCRIPTION OF EACH]

5.1.3 Documentation Software

The following software is required for documentation.
[LIST OF DOCUMENTATION SOFTWARE
AND BRIEF DESCRIPTION OF EACH]

5.1.4 Documentation Facilities

The following facilities are required for documentation.
[LIST OF DOCUMENTATION FACILITIES
AND BRIEF DESCRIPTION OF EACH]

5.1.5 Documentation Schedule

The following milestones are required for documentation.
[LIST OF DOCUMENTATION MILESTONES
AND BRIEF DESCRIPTION OF EACH]
[DOCUMENTATION MILESTONE CHART]
Figure n. Documentation Schedule

5.2 Training Resources

The following subsections describe resources required for training development and implementation in terms of personnel, equipment, software, facilities, and schedule.

5.2.1 Training Personnel

The following types and number of personnel are required for training.
[LIST OF TRAINING PERSONNEL
AND NUMBER REQUIRED]

5.2.2 Training Equipment

The following equipment is required for training.
[LIST OF TRAINING EQUIPMENT
AND BRIEF DESCRIPTION OF EACH]

5.2.3 Training Software

The following software is required for training.
[LIST OF TRAINING SOFTWARE
AND BRIEF DESCRIPTION OF EACH]

5.2.4 Training Facilities

The following facilities are required for training.
[LIST OF TRAINING FACILITIES
AND BRIEF DESCRIPTION OF EACH]

5.2.5 Training Schedule

The following milestones are required for training.
[LIST OF TRAINING MILESTONES
AND BRIEF DESCRIPTION OF EACH]
[TRAINING MILESTONE CHART]
Figure n. Training Schedule

5.3 Customer Support Resources

The following subsections describe resources required for customer support in terms of personnel, equipment, software, facilities, and schedule.

5.3.1 Customer Support Personnel

The following types and number of personnel are required for customer support.
[LIST OF CUSTOMER SUPPORT PERSONNEL
TYPES AND NUMBER REQUIRED]

5.3.2 Customer Support Equipment

The following equipment is required for customer support.
[LIST OF CUSTOMER SUPPORT EQUIPMENT
AND BRIEF DESCRIPTION OF EACH]

5.3.3 Customer Support Software

The following software is required for customer support.
[LIST OF CUSTOMER SUPPORT SOFTWARE
AND BRIEF DESCRIPTION OF EACH]

5.3.4 Customer Support Facilities

The following facilities are required for customer support.
[LIST OF CUSTOMER SUPPORT FACILITIES
AND BRIEF DESCRIPTION OF EACH]

5.3.5 Customer Support Schedule

The following milestones are required for customer support.
[LIST OF CUSTOMER SUPPORT MILESTONES
AND BRIEF DESCRIPTION OF EACH]
[CUSTOMER SUPPORT MILESTONE CHART]
Figure n. Customer Support Schedule

6. DELIVERY RESOURCE REQUIREMENTS

The following subsections describe resources required for delivery in terms of manufacturing and distribution.

6.1 Manufacturing Resources

The following subsections describe resources required for manufacturing in terms of personnel, equipment, software, facilities, and schedule.

6.1.1 Manufacturing Personnel

The following types and number of personnel are required for manufacturing.
[LIST OF MANUFACTURING PERSONNEL
AND NUMBER REQUIRED]

6.1.2 Manufacturing Equipment

The following equipment is required for manufacturing.
[LIST OF MANUFACTURING EQUIPMENT
AND BRIEF DESCRIPTION OF EACH]

6.1.3 Manufacturing Software

The following software is required for manufacturing.
[LIST OF MANUFACTURING SOFTWARE
AND BRIEF DESCRIPTION OF EACH]

6.1.4 Manufacturing Facilities

The following facilities are required for manufacturing.
[LIST OF MANUFACTURING FACILITIES
AND BRIEF DESCRIPTION OF EACH]

6.1.5 Manufacturing Schedule

The following milestones are required for manufacturing.
[LIST OF MANUFACTURING MILESTONES
AND BRIEF DESCRIPTION OF EACH]
[MANUFACTURING MILESTONE CHART]
Figure n. Manufacturing Schedule

6.2 Distribution Resources

The following subsections describe resources required for distribution
in terms of personnel, equipment, software, facilities, and schedule.

6.2.1 Distribution Personnel

The following types and number of personnel are required for distribution.
[LIST OF DISTRIBUTION PERSONNEL
AND NUMBER REQUIRED]

6.2.2 Distribution Equipment

The following equipment is required for distribution.
[LIST OF DISTRIBUTION EQUIPMENT
AND BRIEF DESCRIPTION OF EACH]

6.2.3 Distribution Software

The following software is required for distribution.
[LIST OF DISTRIBUTION SOFTWARE
AND BRIEF DESCRIPTION OF EACH]

6.2.4 Distribution Facilities

The following facilities are required for distribution.
[LIST OF DISTRIBUTION FACILITIES
AND BRIEF DESCRIPTION OF EACH]

6.2.5 Distribution Schedule

The following milestones are required for distribution.
[LIST OF DISTRIBUTION MILESTONES
AND BRIEF DESCRIPTION OF EACH]
[DISTRIBUTION MILESTONE CHART]
Figure n. Distribution Schedule

([APPENDIX TITLE]

The following information details [SUBJECT OF APPENDIX].
[TEXT OF APPENDIX])

GLOSSARY

The following terms and acronyms are used throughout [SYSTEM
ID] documentation.
[LIST OF TERMS AND ACRONYMS
AND THEIR DEFINITIONS]

PART III
CONTROLLING
THE PROJECT

Masters for controlling the project include:
    MANAGEMENT PLAN
    ENGINEERING CHANGE PROPOSAL

7 Management Plan

5. VERIFICATION PLANS

5.1   Responsibilities
5.2   Review Panels
   5.2.n   [VERIFICATION REVIEW PANEL NAME]
5.3   Structure
   5.3.1   Formal Testing
      5.3.1.1   Test Control
      5.3.1.2   Test Classes
      5.3.1.3   Test Levels
   5.3.2   Quality Assurance
   (5.3.n   [ADDITIONAL VERIFICATION FUNCTION])
5.4   High Risk Areas

6. CUSTOMER SERVICES PLANS

6.1   Responsibilities
6.2   Review Panels
   6.2.n   [CUSTOMER SERVICES REVIEW PANEL NAME]
6.3   Structure
   6.3.1   Documentation
   6.3.2   Training
      6.3.2.1   Internal Training
      6.3.2.2   External Training
   6.3.3   Customer Support
   (6.3.n   [ADDITIONAL CUSTOMER SERVICES FUNCTION])
6.4   High Risk Areas

7. DELIVERY PLANS

7.1   Responsibilities
7.2   Review Panels
   7.2.n   [DELIVERY REVIEW PANEL NAME]
7.3   Structure
   7.3.1   Manufacturing
   7.3.2   Distribution
   7.3.3   Installation
   (7.3.n   [ADDITIONAL DELIVERY FUNCTION])
7.4   High Risk Areas

8. MASTER SCHEDULE

9. MASTER COST ANALYSIS

10. RISK MANAGEMENT

10.1 High Risk Milestones

10.2 Recovery Plans

10.2.1 Schedule

10.2.2 Costs

([APPENDIX])

GLOSSARY

1. SCOPE

The following subsections describe the scope of this [SYSTEM ID] Management Plan (MP) in terms of its purpose, audience, organization, and applicable documents.

1.1 Purpose

This MP provides information for control of the [SYSTEM ID] project.

1.2 Audience

The intended users of this MP are [USER TITLES] (with [PRE-REQUISITE KNOWLEDGE].)

1.3 Organization

This MP describes the management plans in terms of:
[DOCUMENT ORGANIZATION DESCRIPTION]

1.4 Applicable Documents

The following documents provide information necessary to understanding this MP.
[SYSTEM ID] System Requirement Specification
[SYSTEM ID] Resource Requirements Specification
([LIST OF OTHER APPLICABLE DOCUMENTS])

2. LIFE-CYCLE MILESTONE NETWORK

The following figure illustrates the project life-cycle milestone network.
[PROJECT LIFE-CYCLE MILESTONE NETWORK]
Figure n. Project Milestone Network

3. PROJECT MANAGEMENT PLANS

The following subsections describe the plans for project management throughout the product life-cycle in terms of:

1. Responsibilities
2. Review panels
3. Structure

3.1 Responsibilities

The following describes the project management responsibilities.
[PRIORITIZED LIST OF MANAGEMENT
RESPONSIBILITIES]

3.2 Review Panels

The following subsections describe project management review panels
throughout the life-cycle in terms of:

1. Purpose
2. Initiation
3. Meeting schedules

3.2.n [MANAGEMENT REVIEW PANEL NAME]

Purpose:

[PURPOSE OF PANEL]

Initiation:

[MEETING INITIATION CONDITIONS]

Meeting Schedule:

[MEETING SCHEDULE]

3.3 Structure

The following figure illustrates the project management organization in
terms of function and reporting structure.
[PROJECT MANAGEMENT ORGANIZATION CHART]
Figure n. Project Management Organization

4. SYSTEM DEVELOPMENT PLANS

The following subsections describe the plans for system development in terms of:

1. Responsibilities
2. Review panels
3. Structure
4. High risk areas

4.1 Responsibilities

The following describes the system development responsibilities.
[PRIORITIZED LIST OF DEVELOPMENT RESPONSIBILITIES]

4.2 Review Panels

The following subsections describe system development review panels throughout the life-cycle in terms of:

1. Purpose
2. Initiation
3. Meeting schedules

4.2.n [DEVELOPMENT REVIEW PANEL NAME]

Purpose:

[PURPOSE OF PANEL]

Initiation:

[MEETING INITIATION CONDITIONS]

Meeting Schedule:

[MEETING SCHEDULE]

4.3 Structure

The following figure illustrates the system development organization in terms of function and reporting structure.

[SYSTEM DEVELOPMENT ORGANIZATION CHART]

Figure n. System Development Organization

The following subsections describe the system development functional organization plans in terms of:

1. Configuration management
2. Development support environment
3. Architectural design
4. Detailed design and implementation

(n. [ADDITIONAL DEVELOPMENT FUNCTION])

4.3.1 Configuration Management

The following subsections describe the plans for configuration management in terms of:

1. Configuration identification
2. Configuration status accounting
3. Configuration audits

4.3.1.1 Configuration Identification

The following describes the plans for identification of system elements and documentation to be put under configuration control.

[CONFIGURATION IDENTIFICATION DESCRIPTION]

4.3.1.2 Configuration Status Accounting

The following describes the plans for status accounting of system elements and documentation under configuration control.

[CONFIGURATION STATUS ACCOUNTING DESCRIPTION]

4.3.1.3 Configuration Audits

The following describes the plans for configuration audit procedures, including Engineering Change Proposals (ECPs).
[CONFIGURATION AUDIT PROCEDURE
DESCRIPTION]

4.3.2 Development Support Environment

The following describes the plans for the development support environment.
[DEVELOPMENT SUPPORT ENVIRONMENT
PLAN DESCRIPTION]

4.3.3 Architectural Design
The following describes the plans for developing the architectural design of the system.
[ARCHITECTURAL DESIGN PLAN DESCRIPTION]

4.3.4 Detailed Design & Implementation

The following describes the plans for developing the detailed design and implementation for the system.
[DETAILED DESIGN AND IMPLEMENTATION
PLAN DESCRIPTION]

(4.3.n [ADDITIONAL DEVELOPMENT FUNCTION]

The following describes the [FUNCTIONAL ORGANIZATION DESCRIPTION].)

4.4 High Risk Areas

The following describes high risk areas in the system development plans.
[LIST OF HIGH RISK AREAS
IN DEVELOPMENT PLANS]

5. VERIFICATION PLANS

The following subsections describe the plans for verification in terms of:

1. Responsibilities
2. Review panels
3. Structure
4. High risk areas

5.1 Responsibilities

The following describes the verification responsibilities.
[PRIORITIZED LIST OF VERIFICATION RESPONSIBILITIES]

5.2 Review Panels

The following subsections describe verification review panels throughout the life-cycle in terms of:

1. Purpose
2. Initiation
3. Meeting schedules

5.2.n [VERIFICATION REVIEW PANEL NAME]

Purpose:

[PURPOSE OF PANEL]

Initiation:

[MEETING INITIATION CONDITIONS]

Meeting Schedule:

[MEETING SCHEDULE]

5.3 Structure

The following figure illustrates the verification organization in terms of function and reporting structure.

[VERIFICATION ORGANIZATION CHART]

Figure n. Verification Organization

The following subsections describe the system verification functional organization plans in terms of:

1. Formal testing
2. Quality assurance
(n. [ADDITIONAL VERIFICATION FUNCTION])

5.3.1 Formal Testing

The following subsections describe plans for formal testing in terms of:

1. Test control
2. Test classes
3. Test levels

5.3.1.1 Test Control

The following describes the procedures for test control.

[TEST CONTROL PROCEDURES DESCRIPTION]

5.3.1.2 Test Classes

The following describes the classes of formal tests (for example, timing tests, capacity tests, error recovery tests).

[LIST AND DESCRIPTIONS OF TEST CLASSES]

5.3.1.3 Test Levels

The following describes the levels at which formal tests will be performed.

[LIST AND DESCRIPTIONS OF TEST LEVELS]

5.3.2 Quality Assurance

The following subsections describe the procedures for quality assurance.

Design Document Evaluation:

[DESIGN DOCUMENT EVALUATION PROCEDURE]

Configuration Management Evaluation:

[CONFIGURATION MANAGEMENT
EVALUATION PROCEDURE]

Design Standards Evaluation:

[DESIGN STANDARDS EVALUATION PROCEDURE]

Design Implementation Evaluation:

[DESIGN IMPLEMENTATION EVALUATION
PROCEDURE]

Test Performance Evaluation:

[TEST PERFORMANCE EVALUATION PROCEDURE]

End-user Document Evaluation:

[END-USER EVALUATION PROCEDURE]

Manufacturing and Distribution Evaluation:

[MANUFACTURING AND DISTRIBUTION
EVALUATION PROCEDURE]

(5.3.n [ADDITIONAL VERIFICATION FUNCTION]

The following describes the [FUNCTIONAL ORGANIZATION
DESCRIPTION].)

5.4 High Risk Areas

The following describes high risk areas in the verification plans.
[LIST OF HIGH RISK AREAS IN VERIFICATION PLANS]

6. CUSTOMER SERVICES PLANS

The following subsections describe the plans for customer services in terms of:

1. Responsibilities
2. Review panels
3. Structure
4. High risk areas

6.1 Responsibilities

The following describes the customer services responsibilities.
[PRIORITIZED LIST OF CUSTOMER SERVICES RESPONSIBILITIES]

6.2 Review Panels

The following subsections describe customer service review panels throughout the life-cycle in terms of:

1. Purpose
2. Initiation
3. Meeting schedules

6.2.n [CUSTOMER SERVICES REVIEW PANEL NAME]

Purpose:
[PURPOSE OF PANEL]

Initiation:
[MEETING INITIATION CONDITIONS]

Meeting Schedule:
[MEETING SCHEDULE]

6.3 Structure

The following figure illustrates the customer services organization in terms of function and reporting structure.

[CUSTOMER SERVICES ORGANIZATION CHART]

Figure n. Customer Services Organization

The following subsections describe the customer services functional organization plans in terms of:

1. Documentation
2. Training
3. Customer support
(4. [ADDITIONAL CUSTOMER SERVICES FUNCTION])

6.3.1 Documentation

The following describes the plans for documentation throughout the life-cycle, including a list of required end-user documents.

[DOCUMENTATION PLANS DESCRIPTION]

[LIST OF END-USER DOCUMENTS]

6.3.2 Training

The following subsections describe the plans for internal and external training.

6.3.2.1 Internal Training

The following describes internal training.

Trainers:

[TRAINER SKILLS DESCRIPTION]

Trainees:

[PROSPECTIVE TRAINEE DESCRIPTION]

Training Methods:

[TRAINING METHODS DESCRIPTION]

Duration of Training:

[DURATION OF TRAINING]

6.3.2.2 External Training

The following describes external, end-user training.

Trainers:

[TRAINER SKILLS DESCRIPTION]

Trainees:

[PROSPECTIVE TRAINEE DESCRIPTION]

Training Methods:

[TRAINING METHODS DESCRIPTION]

Duration of Training:

[DURATION OF TRAINING]

6.3.3 Customer Support

The following describes procedures for customer support.

Scheduled Maintenance:

[SCHEDULED MAINTENANCE PROCEDURES]

Customer Call Handling:

[CUSTOMER CALL HANDLING PROCEDURES]

Escalation Scheme:

[ESCALATION SCHEME DESCRIPTION]

Follow Up:

[FOLLOW UP PROCEDURES]

Scheduled User Updates:

[LIST AND DESCRIPTION OF USER UPDATE DOCUMENTS]

(6.3.n [ADDITIONAL CUSTOMER SERVICES FUNCTION]

The following describes the [FUNCTIONAL ORGANIZATION DESCRIPTION].)

6.4 High Risk Areas

The following describes high risk areas in the customer service plans.
[LIST OF HIGH RISK AREAS IN
CUSTOMER SERVICES PLANS]

7. DELIVERY PLANS

The following subsections describe the plans for delivery in terms of:

1. Responsibilities
2. Review Panels
3. Structure
4. High risk areas

7.1 Responsibilities

The following describes the delivery responsibilities.
[PRIORITIZED LIST OF DELIVERY RESPONSIBILITIES]

7.2 Review Panels

The following subsections describe delivery review panels throughout the life-cycle in terms of:

1. Purpose
2. Initiation
3. Meeting schedules

7.2.n [DELIVERY REVIEW PANEL NAME]

Purpose:

[PURPOSE OF PANEL]

Initiation:

[MEETING INITIATION CONDITIONS]

Meeting Schedule:

[MEETING SCHEDULE]

7.3 Structure

The following figure illustrates the delivery organization in terms of function and reporting structure.

[DELIVERY ORGANIZATION CHART]

Figure n. Delivery Organization

The following subsections describe the delivery functional organization plans in terms of:

1. Manufacturing
2. Distribution
3. Installation
(n. [ADDITIONAL DELIVERY FUNCTION])

7.3.1 Manufacturing

The following describes the procedures for manufacturing the system.

Classification:

[CLASSIFICATION DESCRIPTION]

Labeling:

[LABELING DESCRIPTION]

Packaging:

[PACKAGING DESCRIPTION]

7.3.2 Distribution

The following describes the procedures for distribution of the system and its documentation.

Handling:

[HANDLING DESCRIPTION]

Required Documentation:

[LIST OF REQUIRED DOCUMENTATION]

Optional Documentation:

[LIST OF OPTIONAL DOCUMENTATION]

7.3.3 Installation

The following describes the procedures for installing the system.
[INSTALLATION PROCEDURE DESCRIPTION]

(7.3.n [ADDITIONAL DELIVERY FUNCTION]

The following describes the [FUNCTIONAL ORGANIZATION DESCRIPTION].)

7.4 High Risk Areas

The following describes high risk areas in the delivery plans.
[LIST OF HIGH RISK AREAS IN DELIVERY PLANS]

8. MASTER SCHEDULE

The following figure illustrates the Master Schedule of major project milestones throughout the system life-cycle.
[MASTER MILESTONE CHART]
Figure n. [SYSTEM ID] Life-Cycle Master Schedule

9. MASTER COST ANALYSIS

The following summarizes the results of life-cycle cost analysis.
[COST ANALYSIS RESULTS DESCRIPTION]

10. RISK MANAGEMENT

The following describes project life-cycle risk management in terms of:

1. High risk milestones
2. Recovery plans

10.1 High Risk Milestones

The following lists and briefly describes the reasons for high risk project milestones.
[LIST AND BRIEF DESCRIPTION OF MILESTONE RISKS]

10.2 Recovery Plans

The following subsections describe project recovery plans in terms of schedule and cost.

10.2.1 Schedule

The following describes the recovery plans for project schedule slips.
[SCHEDULE RECOVERY PLAN DESCRIPTION]

10.2.2 Costs

The following describes the recovery plans for project cost overruns.
[COST RECOVERY PLAN DESCRIPTION]

([APPENDIX TITLE]

The following information details [SUBJECT OF APPENDIX].
[TEXT OF APPENDIX])

GLOSSARY

The following terms and acronyms are used throughout [SYSTEM ID] documentation.
[LIST OF TERMS AND ACRONYMS
AND THEIR DEFINITIONS]

8 Engineering Change Proposal

1. SCOPE

The following subsections describe the scope of this Engineering Change Proposal (ECP) in terms of its purpose, audience, organization, and applicable documents.

1.1 Purpose

This ECP provides information for initiating and resolving an engineering change.

1.2 Audience

The intended users of this ECP are [USER TITLES] (with [PRE-REQUISITE KNOWLEDGE]).

1.3 Organization

This ECP describes engineering changes in terms of:
     [DOCUMENT ORGANIZATION DESCRIPTION]

1.4 Applicable Documents

The following documents provide information necessary to understanding this ECP.
     [SYSTEM ID] Management Plan
     [LIST OF OTHER APPLICABLE DOCUMENTS]

2. ENGINEERING CHANGE PROCEDURES

The following figure illustrates the process by which engineering changes are initiated and resolved.

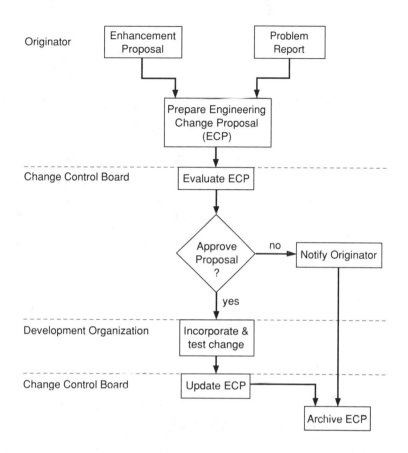

3. ECP FORM DEFINITION

The following figure illustrates the Engineering Change Proposal (ECP) Form that must accompany each change to the system design or project scope that is proposed.

The Form fields are described below the Form.

1. ECP NUMBER : _____

To be filled in by originator.

2. SYSTEM / PROJECT ID : _____

3. ORIGINATOR : _____   **4. SUBMITTAL DATE :** __/__/__

5. PROBLEM / ENHANCEMENT SUMMARY : _____

_____

_____

_____

6. AREAS AFFECTED : _____

_____

_____

_____

_____

7. NEED DATE : __/__/__

8. PROBLEM / ENHANCEMENT DESCRIPTION : _____

_____

_____

_____

_____

_____

_____

_____

(Use additional sheets if necessary)

To be filled in by authorized members of the CCB.

9. **DATE ASSIGNED :** __/__/__   10. **ASSIGNED TO :** _____

11. **DATE COMPLETED :** __/__/__

12. **RECOMMENDED SOLUTION :**   YES / NO

SUMMARY OF SOLUTION : _____

_____

_____

_____

13. **IMPACTS OF SOLUTION :** _____

_____

COST : _____

_____

SCHEDULE : _____

_____

RESOURCES : _____

_____

PERFORMANCE : _____

_____

_____

_____

_____

_____

(Use additional sheets if necessary)

−2−

14. **APPROVAL OF SOLUTION**

        NAME : _____

        TITLE : _____

15. **PRIORITY :** _____

16. **IMPLEMENTATION SCHEDULE :** __/__/__ to __/__/__

17. **IMPLEMENTOR**
        NAME : _____

        TITLE : _____

18. **IMPLEMENTATION COMPLETION :** __/__/__

19. **VERIFICATION**

        NAME : _____

        TITLE : _____   **DATE :** __/__/__

20. **IMPACTS OF IMPLEMENTATION :** _____

_____

_____

_____

_____

_____

_____

_____

_____

21. **VERSION NUMBER :** _____

The following defines the ECP Form fields.

1. **ECP NUMBER:** The number of the problem or enhancement proposal, assigned by the Change Control Board (CCB) administration.

2. **SYSTEM/PROJECT ID:** The identifier of the system or project to which this problem or enhancement applies.

3. **ORIGINATOR:** The name and title of the person submitting the ECP.

4. **SUBMITTAL DATE:** The date that the ECP Form is submitted to the CCB administration.

5. **PROBLEM/ENHANCEMENT SUMMARY:** A brief description of the problem/enhancement.

6. **AREAS AFFECTED:** The specific system component(s), documents, and/or organizations that will be affected by the problem fix or enhancement.

7. **NEED DATE:** The time by which the fix/enhancement is needed in order not to delay schedules.

8. **PROBLEM/ENHANCEMENT DESCRIPTION:** Analysis of the problem/enhancement, including conditions on inputs, processing, outputs, testing, and relationship to other reported problems or modifications.

9. **DATE ASSIGNED:** The date that the proposed change is assigned for CCB analysis and evaluation.

10. **ASSIGNED TO:** The name and title of the CCB member or analyst assigned to evaluate the proposed change.

11. **DATE COMPLETED:** The date the evaluation of the proposed change is completed and submitted.

12. **RECOMMENDED SOLUTION:** The solution to the evaluation of the proposed change (YES/NO) and if YES, then a summary of the solution.

13. **IMPACTS OF SOLUTION:** If the solution is YES, then predicted cost, schedule, resource, and system performance impacts. If the solution is NO, then predicted system performance impacts.

14. **APPROVAL OF SOLUTION:** The name and title of the person with authority of approval.

15. **PRIORITY:** The priority of the change according to CCB classifications.

16. **IMPLEMENTATION SCHEDULE:** The dates when implementation of the change is to begin and end.

17. **IMPLEMENTOR:** The name and title of the person assigned to implement the change.

18. **IMPLEMENTATION COMPLETION:** The actual date of change implementation completion.

19. **VERIFICATION:** The name and title of the person who tested the implementation and the date of its verification.

20. **IMPACTS OF IMPLEMENTATION:** Actual cost, schedule, resource, and performance impacts realized, including any differences from impacts predicted in Field 13.

21. **VERSION NUMBER:** The system version in which the change will be incorporated.

([APPENDIX TITLE]

The following information details [SUBJECT OF APPENDIX].
        [TEXT OF APPENDIX])

GLOSSARY

The following terms and acronyms are used throughout [SYSTEM ID] documentation.
        [LIST OF TERMS AND ACRONYMS
        AND THEIR DEFINITIONS]

PART IV
DEVELOPING THE SYSTEM

Masters for describing the product development include:

ARCHITECTURE DESIGN DOCUMENT
PROTOTYPE DESIGN DOCUMENT
DETAILED DESIGN DOCUMENT
TEST SPECIFICATIONS
TEST REPORTS

9 Architecture Design Document

1. SCOPE

    1.1 Purpose
    1.2 Audience
    1.3 Organization
    1.4 Applicable Documents

2. REQUIREMENTS IMPLEMENTATION

3. ARCHITECTURE & INFRASTRUCTURE

    3.n [NAME] Top-Level Module
       3.n.1 Interfaces
       3.n.n [NAME] Sublevel Module
          3.n.n.1 Function
          3.n.n.2 Interfaces
          3.n.n.3 Control
          3.n.n.4 Error Recovery

4. DESIGN STANDARDS

    4.1 Methodology
    4.2 Programming Language(s)
    4.3 Interface Standards
    4.4 Naming Conventions

([APPENDIX])

GLOSSARY

1. SCOPE

The following subsections describe the scope of this [SYSTEM ID] Architecture Design Document (ADD) in terms of its purpose, audience, organization, and applicable documents.

1.1 Purpose

This ADD provides information for [PURPOSE OF ADD IN TERMS OF SPECIFICATIONS FURTHER DEVELOPMENT].

1.2 Audience

The intended users of this ADD are [USER TITLES] (with [PREREQUISITE KNOWLEDGE]).

1.3 Organization

This ADD describes the [SYSTEM ID] architecture in terms of:
     [DOCUMENT ORGANIZATION DESCRIPTION]

1.4 Applicable Documents

The following documents provide information necessary to understanding this ADD.
     [SYSTEM ID] System Requirements Specification
     [LIST OF OTHER APPLICABLE DOCUMENTS]

2. REQUIREMENTS IMPLEMENTATION

The following Requirements Cross-Reference Table maps each [SYSTEM ID] top-level module to the requirements it fulfills in the *[SYSTEM ID] System Requirements Specification*.
          Table n. Requirements Cross Reference
               [CROSS REFERENCE TABLE]

3. ARCHITECTURE & INFRASTRUCTURE

The following block diagram illustrates the system in terms of its top-level major functional modules and interfaces.

[FUNCTIONAL BLOCK DIAGRAM]

Figure n. [SYSTEM ID] Functions and Interfaces

The following subsections describe the system architecture and infrastructure in terms of top-level functional modules.

3.n [NAME] Top-Level Module

The following block diagram illustrates [NAME] top-level module in terms of its interfaces and sublevel modules.

[TOP-LEVEL MODULE BLOCK DIAGRAM]

Figure n. [NAME] Top-Level Module

The following subsections describe the [NAME] top-level module in terms of:

1. Interfaces

2. Sublevel modules

3.n.1 Interfaces

The following [NAME] Top-Level Module Interface Table describes the interfaces in terms of:

1. Identifier

2. Purpose

3. Concurrent or sequential nature

4. Transfer protocol

5. Initiating conditions

6. Completion conditions

Table n. [NAME] Top-Level Module Interface Table
[TOP-LEVEL MODULE INTERFACE TABLE]

3.n.n [NAME] Sublevel Module

The following subsections describe architectural design of the [NAME] sublevel module in terms of:

1. Function
2. Interface
3. Control
4. Error recovery

3.n.n.1 Function

The following describes the function(s) of the [NAME] sublevel module.
   [SUBLEVEL MODULE FUNCTIONAL DESCRIPTION]

3.n.n.2 Interfaces

The following [NAME] Sublevel Module Interface Table describes the interfaces in terms of:

1. Identifier
2. Purpose
3. Source/destination
4. Size
5. Limit/range
6. Accuracy/precision
7. Frequency
8. Legality checks

   Table n. [NAME] Sublevel Module Interface Table
      [SUBLEVEL MODULE INTERFACE TABLE]

3.n.n.3 Control

The following describes the control structure of the [NAME] sublevel module.
      [SUBLEVEL MODULE CONTROL STRUCTURE DESCRIPTION]

3.n.n.4 Error Recovery

The following describes error recovery in the [NAME] sublevel module.
> [SUBLEVEL MODULE ERROR RECOVERY DESCRIPTION]

4. DESIGN STANDARDS

The following subsections define the coding standards to be used for detailed design and implementation of the system, module, and unit level functions in terms of:

1. Methodology
2. Programming languages
3. Interface rules and standards
4. Naming conventions

4.1 Methodology

The following describes the design methodology and its implications.
> [DESIGN METHODOLOGY DESCRIPTION]

4.2 Programming Language(s)

The following describes the programming languages to be used and the rationale for their use.
> [LIST OF LANGUAGE CHOICES & RATIONALES]

4.3 Interface Standards

The following describes standards for consistency of interfaces.

Displays:
> [LIST OF DISPLAY STANDARDS]

Commands:
> [COMMAND NAMING STANDARDS]

Function Keys:

[LIST OF STANDARD KEY FUNCTIONS]

Entries to Programs/Utilities:

[ENTRY STANDARD]

Exits from Programs/Utilities:

[EXIT STANDARD]

4.4 Naming Conventions

The following describes system element naming conventions.

Modules:

[MODULE NAMING CONVENTIONS]

Units:

[UNIT NAMING CONVENTIONS]

Interfaces:

[INTERFACE NAMING CONVENTIONS]

([APPENDIX TITLE]

The following information details [SUBJECT OF APPENDIX].
[TEXT OF APPENDIX])

GLOSSARY

The following terms and acronyms are used throughout [SYSTEM ID] documentation.
[LIST OF TERMS AND ACRONYMS
AND THEIR DEFINITIONS]

10 Prototype Design Document

1. SCOPE

    1.1 Purpose

    1.2 Audience

    1.3 Organization

    1.4 Applicable Documents

2. FUNCTION(S)

3. DESIGN & IMPLEMENTATION

    3.n [NAME] Top-Level Module

        3.n.1 Interfaces

        3.n.n [NAME] Sublevel Module

            3.n.n.1 Function

            3.n.n.2 Control

([APPENDIXES])

GLOSSARY

1. SCOPE

The following subsections describe the scope of this [SYSTEM ID] Prototype Design Document (PDD) in terms of its purpose, audience, organization, and applicable documents.

1.1 Purpose

This PDD provides information for [PURPOSE OF PDD IN TERMS OF PREVIOUS AND FURTHER DEVELOPMENT].

1.2 Audience

The intended users of this PDD are [USER TITLES] (with [PRE-REQUISITE KNOWLEDGE]).

1.3 Organization

This PDD describes the [NAME] Prototype for [SYSTEM ID] in terms of:
[DOCUMENT ORGANIZATION DESCRIPTION]

1.4 Applicable Documents

The following documents provide information necessary to understanding this PDD.
[SYSTEM ID] System Requirement Specification
[SYSTEM ID] Architecture Design Document
[LIST OF OTHER APPLICABLE DOCUMENTS]

2. FUNCTION(S)

The following block diagram illustrates the prototype in terms of its major functional modules and interfaces.
[FUNCTIONAL BLOCK DIAGRAM]
Figure n. [NAME] Prototype Functions and Interfaces

3. DESIGN & IMPLEMENTATION

The following subsections describe design of the [NAME] prototype top-level modules.

3.n [NAME] Top-Level Module

The following block diagram illustrates the [NAME] top-level module in terms of its interfaces and sublevel modules.

[TOP-LEVEL BLOCK DIAGRAM]

Figure n. [NAME] Top-Level Module

The following subsections describe the [NAME] top-level module in terms of:

1. Interfaces
2. Sublevel modules

3.n.1 Interfaces

The following [NAME] Top-Level Module Interface Table describes the interface in terms of:

1. Identifier
2. Purpose
3. Implementation

Table n. [NAME] Top-Level Module Interface Table
[TOP-LEVEL MODULE INTERFACE TABLE]

3.n.n [NAME] Sublevel Module

The following subsections describe the [NAME] sublevel module in terms of function and control.

3.n.n.1 Function

The following describes the function(s) of the [NAME] sublevel module.

[MODULE FUNCTIONAL DESCRIPTION]

3.n.n.2 Control

The following describes the control structure of the [NAME] sublevel module.
   [MODULE CONTROL STRUCTURE DESCRIPTION]

([APPENDIX TITLE]

The following information details [SUBJECT OF APPENDIX].
         [TEXT OF APPENDIX])

GLOSSARY

The following terms and acronyms are used throughout [SYSTEM ID] documentation.
         [LIST OF TERMS AND ACRONYMS
         AND THEIR DEFINITIONS]

11 Detailed Design Document

1. SCOPE

The following subsections describe the scope of this [SYSTEM ID] Detailed Design Document (DDD) in terms of its purpose, audience, organization, and applicable documents.

1.1 Purpose

This DDD provides information for [PURPOSE OF DDD IN TERMS OF IMPLEMENTATION].

1.2 Audience

The intended users of this DDD are [USER TITLES] (with PRE-REQUISITE KNOWLEDGE]).

1.3 Organization

This DDD describes the [SYSTEM ID] detailed design in terms of:
     [DOCUMENT ORGANIZATION DESCRIPTION]

1.4 Applicable Documents

The following documents provide information necessary to understanding this [DOCUMENT IDENTIFICATION].
     [SYSTEM ID] System Requirements Specification
     [SYSTEM ID] Architecture Design Document
     ([SYSTEM ID] Prototype Design Document)
     [LIST OF OTHER APPLICABLE DOCUMENTS]

2. ARCHITECTURE & INFRASTRUCTURE

The following block diagram illustrates the system architecture and infrastructure in terms of top-level functional modules and interfaces.
     [TOP-LEVEL BLOCK DIAGRAM]
     Figure n. Top-Level Block Diagram
The following subsections describe detailed design of (and/or changes to) the top-level module design.

2.n [NAME] Top-Level Module Design

[TOP-LEVEL MODULE DESIGN/CHANGE DESCRIPTION]

3. DETAILED DESIGN & IMPLEMENTATION

The following subsections describe detailed design of the sublevel modules.

3.n [NAME] Sublevel Module Design

The following block diagram illustrates the [NAME] sublevel module in terms of its functional units.

[SUBLEVEL BLOCK DIAGRAM]
Figure n. [NAME] Sublevel Block Diagram

3.n.1 Interfaces

The following [NAME] Sublevel Module Interface Table describes the interfaces in terms of:

1. Identifier
2. Purpose
3. Source/destination
4. Size
5. Frequency

Table n. [NAME] Sublevel Module Interface Table
[SUBLEVEL MODULE INTERFACE TABLE]

3.n.n [NAME] Unit Design

The following subsections describe detailed design of the [NAME] unit in terms of:

1. Function
2. Interfaces

3. Control
4. Error handling

3.n.n.1 Function

The following describes the function of the [NAME] unit.
[UNIT FUNCTIONAL DESCRIPTION]

3.n.n.2 Interfaces

The following Unit Interface Table describes the [NAME] unit interfaces in terms of:

1. Identifier
2. Purpose
3. Source/destination
4. Size
5. Data type
6. Data representation
7. Limit/range
8. Accuracy/precision
9. Frequency
10. Legality checks

Table n. [NAME] Unit Interface Table
[UNIT INTERFACE TABLE]

3.n.n.3 Control

The following describes details of the control structure of the [NAME] unit.
[CONTROL STRUCTURE DESCRIPTION]

3.n.n.4 Error Handling

The following describes details of error handling in the [NAME] unit.
[ERROR HANDLING DESCRIPTION]

([APPENDIX TITLE]

The following information details [SUBJECT OF APPENDIX].
[TEXT OF APPENDIX])

GLOSSARY

The following terms and acronyms are used throughout [SYSTEM ID] documentation.
[LIST OF TERMS AND ACRONYMS
AND THEIR DEFINITIONS]

12 Test Specifications

1. SCOPE

The following subsections describe the scope of this [SYSTEM ID] Test Specifications (TS) in terms of its purpose, audience, organization, and applicable documents.

1.1 Purpose

This TS specifies requirements for formal tests of [SYSTEM ID] System.

1.2 Audience

The intended users of this TS are [USER TITLES] (with [PREREQUISITE KNOWLEDGE]).

1.3 Organization

This TS specifies [SYSTEM ID] test requirements in terms of:
    [DOCUMENT ORGANIZATION DESCRIPTION]

1.4 Applicable Documents

The following documents provide information necessary to understanding this TS.
    [SYSTEM ID] System Requirements Specification
    [SYSTEM ID] Management Plan
    [SYSTEM ID] Architecture Design Document
    [SYSTEM ID] Detailed Design Document
    [LIST OF OTHER APPLICABLE DOCUMENTS]

2. TEST CLASSIFICATION

The following describes test classification in terms of:

1. Classes

2. Levels

3. Types

2.1 Classes

The following describes the classes of formal tests.
[LIST AND DESCRIPTION OF TEST CLASSES]

2.2 Levels

The following describes the levels at which formal tests will be performed.
[LIST AND DESCRIPTION OF TEST LEVELS]

2.3 Types

The following subsections summarize the types of tests in terms of:

1. Interface tests
2. Functional tests
3. Performance tests

2.3.1 Interface Tests

The following subsections describe the interface tests in terms of:

1. Equipment interfaces
2. Software interfaces
3. User interfaces

2.3.1.1 Equipment Interfaces

The following Equipment Interface Test Summary Table lists and describes the equipment interface tests in terms of:

1. Identification
2. Class
3. Level
4. [SYSTEM ID] SRS requirement(s) to be tested

Table n. Equipment Interface Test Summary Table
[EQUIPMENT INTERFACE TEST SUMMARY TABLE]

2.3.1.2 Software Interfaces

The following Software Interface Test Summary Table lists and describes the software interface tests in terms of:

1. Identification
2. Class
3. Level
4. [SYSTEM ID] SRS requirement(s) to be tested

Table n. Software Interface Test Summary Table
[SOFTWARE INTERFACE TEST SUMMARY TABLE]

2.3.1.3 User Interfaces

The following User Interface Test Summary Table lists and describes the user interface tests in terms of:

1. Identification
2. Class
3. Level
4. [SYSTEM ID] SRS requirement(s) to be tested

Table n. User Interface Test Summary Table
[USER INTERFACE TEST SUMMARY TABLE]

2.3.2 Functional Tests

The following Functional Test Summary Table lists and describes the functional tests in terms of:

1. Identification
2. Class
3. Level
4. [SYSTEM ID] SRS requirement(s) to be tested

Table n. Functional Test Summary Table
[FUNCTIONAL TEST SUMMARY TABLE]

2.3.3 Performance Tests

The following Performance Test Summary Table lists and describes the performance tests in terms of:

1. Identification
2. Level
3. Class
4. [SYSTEM ID] SRS requirement(s) to be tested

Table n. Performance Test Summary Table
[PERFORMANCE TEST SUMMARY TABLE]

3. INTERFACE TESTS

The following subsections specify each interface test identified in the Interface Summary Tables in terms of:

1. Method
2. Criteria
3. Preparation

4. Procedure

5. Recording

3.n [TEST ID] Interact Test

The following specifies the [TEST ID] interface test.

Method:

[TEST METHOD DESCRIPTION]

Criteria:

[TEST CRITERIA DESCRIPTION]

Preparation:

[STEPS IN PREPARATION PROCEDURE]

Procedure:

[STEPS IN TEST PROCEDURE]

Recording:

The test must be recorded on a copy of the Test Log Form illustrated and described in Section 6 of this TS and in the *Test Reports*.
([OTHER TEST RECORDING SPECIFICATIONS])

4. FUNCTIONAL TESTS

The following subsections specify each functional test identified in the Functional Test Summary Table in terms of:

1. Method

2. Criteria

3. Preparation

4. Procedure

5. Recording

4.n [TEST ID] Functional Test

The following specifies the [TEST ID] functional test.

Method:

[TEST METHOD DESCRIPTION]

Criteria:

[TEST CRITERIA DESCRIPTION]

Preparation:

[STEPS IN TEST PREPARATION PROCEDURE]

Procedure:

[STEPS IN TEST PROCEDURE]

Recording:

The test must be recorded on a copy of the Test Log Form illustrated and described in Section 6 of this TS and in the *Test Reports*.
([OTHER TEST RECORDING SPECIFICATIONS])

5. PERFORMANCE TESTS

The following subsections specify each performance test identified in the Performance Test Summary Table in terms of:

1. Method

2. Criteria

3. Preparation

4. Procedure

5. Recording

5.n [TEST ID] Performance Test

The following specifies the [TEST ID] performance test.

Method:

[TEST METHOD DESCRIPTION]

Criteria:

[TEST CRITERIA DESCRIPTION]

Preparation:

[STEPS IN TEST PREPARATION PROCEDURE]

Procedure:

[STEPS IN TEST PROCEDURE]

Recording:

The test must be recorded on a copy of the Test Log Form illustrated and described in Section 6 of this TS and in the *Test Report*.
([OTHER TEST RECORDING SPECIFICATIONS])

6. TEST LOG DEFINITION

The following figure illustrates the Test Log Form, which is to be filled in for each test described in Sections 3, 4, and 5, above.
Form fields are described below the Form.

1. **TEST ID :** _____   2. **TEST CLASS :** _____

3. **TEST LEVEL :** _____

4. **NAME :** _____

5. **TITLE :** _____   6. **DATE :** __/__/__

7. **HARDWARE CONFIGURATION :** _____

_____

8. **SOFTWARE CONFIGURATION :** _____

_____

9. **DEVIATIONS :** _____

_____

10. **RESULT : (PASS/FAIL)**

11. **TIME**	12. **EVENT**

The following defines the Test Log Form fields.

1. *TEST ID:* The identifier assigned to the test in this TS.
2. *TEST CLASS:* The test class assigned in this TS.
3. *TEST LEVEL:* The test level class assigned in this TS.
4. *NAME:* The name of the person performing the test.
5. *TITLE:* The title of the person performing the test.
6. *DATE:* The date of the test.
7. *HARDWARE CONFIGURATION:* The hardware on which the test is run.
8. *SOFTWARE CONFIGURATION:* The software on which the test is run.
9. *DEVIATIONS:* Any deviations from the test as specified in the TS.
10. *RESULT: PASS/FAIL* One of which is to be circled at the completion of the test.
11. *TIME:* The time at which an event in the test was carried out.
12. *EVENT:* An activity in the test procedure.

([APPENDIX TITLE]

The following information details [SUBJECT OF APPENDIX].
[TEXT OF APPENDIX])

GLOSSARY

The following terms and acronyms are used throughout [SYSTEM ID] documentation.
[LIST OF TERMS AND ACRONYMS
AND THEIR DEFINITIONS]

13 Test Reports

1. **SCOPE**
   1.1 Purpose
   1.2 Audience
   1.3 Organization
   1.4 Applicable Documents
2. **INTERFACE TEST REPORTS**
   2.n [TEST ID] Interface Test
3. **FUNCTIONAL TEST REPORTS**
   3.n [TEST ID] Functional Test
4. **PERFORMANCE TEST REPORTS**
   4.n [TEST ID] Performance Test
APPENDIX A — TEST LOGS
[(APPENDIX])
GLOSSARY

1. SCOPE

The following subsections describe the scope of this [SYSTEM ID] Test Reports (TR) in terms of its purpose, audience, organization, and applicable documents.

1.1 Purpose

This TR provides the results of tests performed on the [SYSTEM ID] System.

1.2 Audience

The intended users of this TR are [USER TITLES] (with [PREREQ-UISITE KNOWLEDGE]).

1.3 Organization

This TR describes the [SYSTEM ID] tests in terms of:
   [DOCUMENTATION ORGANIZATION DESCRIPTION]

1.4 Applicable Documents

The following documents provide information necessary to understanding this TR.
     [SYSTEM ID] Test Specifications
     [LIST OF OTHER APPLICABLE DOCUMENTS]

2. INTERFACE TEST REPORTS

The following subsections describe each interface test in terms of:

1. Result
2. Test Log Summary
3. Recommendation

2.n [TEST ID] Interface Test

Result:

[PASS/FAIL]

Test Log Summary:

[TEST LOG SUMMARY DESCRIPTION]

Recommendation:

[RECOMMENDATION]

3. FUNCTIONAL TEST REPORTS

The following subsections describe each functional test in terms of:

1. Result
2. Test Log Summary
3. Recommendation

3.n [TEST ID] Functional Test

Result:

[PASS/FAIL]

Test Log Summary:

[TEST LOG SUMMARY DESCRIPTION]

Recommendation:

[RECOMMENDATION]

4. PERFORMANCE TEST REPORTS

The following subsections describe each performance test in terms of:

1. Result

2. Test Log Summary

3. Recommendation

4.n [TEST ID] Performance Test

Result:

[PASS/FAIL]

Test Log Summary:

[TEST LOG SUMMARY DESCRIPTION]

Recommendation:

[RECOMMENDATION]

APPENDIX A — TEST LOGS

The following [describes/references] test logs.
[TEXT OF APPENDIX]

([APPENDIX TITLE]

The following information details [SUBJECT OF APPENDIX].
[TEXT OF APPENDIX])

GLOSSARY

The following terms and acronyms are used throughout [SYSTEM ID] documentation.
[LIST OF TERMS AND ACRONYMS
AND THEIR DEFINITIONS]

PART V
DELIVERING THE SYSTEM

Masters to accompany the system delivery include:

USERS GUIDE
RELEASE DESCRIPTION
SYSTEM ADMINISTRATORS GUIDE
REFERENCE GUIDE
ACCEPTANCE SIGNOFF

14 Users Guide

PREFACE

The following describes this users guide in terms of purpose, audience, organization, and related documentation.

Purpose

This *[PRODUCT NAME] Users Guide* provides information and procedures to use the [PRODUCT NAME] System.

Audience

The intended users of this guide are [USER TITLES] (with [PRE-REQUISITE KNOWLEDGE]).

Organization

This guide describes [PRODUCT NAME] in terms of:
    [DOCUMENT ORGANIZATION DESCRIPTION]

Documentation

Related documentation includes:
    [LIST OF APPLICABLE DOCUMENTS]

COMMAND SYNTAX NOTATION

The following table lists and describes notation used throughout [PRODUCT NAME] publications to illustrate command syntax.

NOTATION	MEANING
[SYMBOL]	Required as shown
[SYMBOL]	Required
[SYMBOL]	Optional
[SYMBOL]	Choice
•••	Repeat
[SYMBOL]	[MEANING]

Examples:

SYNTAX: [COMMAND AS SHOWN IN GUIDE]

COMMAND: [COMMAND AS ENTERED BY USER]

SYNTAX: [COMMAND AS SHOWN IN GUIDE]

COMMAND: [COMMAND AS ENTERED BY USER]

NOTE: Any commands that do not conform to the above notation are identified in text.

1. INTRODUCTION

This chapter introduces [PRODUCT NAME].
    [USE(S)/FEATURES DESCRIPTION]

1.1 Configurations

The following describes the configurations under which [PRODUCT NAME] runs.
    [(LIST OF) CONFIGURATION DESCRIPTION(S)]

1.2 Function Flow

The following figure illustrates the functional flow of [PRODUCT NAME].
    [FUNCTION FLOW DIAGRAM]
    Figure n. [PRODUCT NAME] Functional Flow

2. USER INTERFACE

This chapter describes the user interfaces to [PRODUCT NAME] in terms of:

1. Display screens
2. Command types

2.1 Display Screens

The following describes [PRODUCT NAME] display screen organization and uses.
[DISPLAY SCREEN DESCRIPTION]

2.2 Command Types

The following describes [PRODUCT NAME] command usage types.
[COMMAND TYPES DESCRIPTION]

3. GETTING STARTED

This chapter contains basic procedures to help you get started using [PRODUCT NAME].

3.1 Login

The following describes [PRODUCT NAME] login procedures.
[STEPS IN LOGIN PROCEDURES]

3.2 Logout

The following describes [PRODUCT NAME] logout procedures.
[STEPS IN LOGOUT PROCEDURES]

3.3 Save

The following describes [PRODUCT NAME] save procedures.
[STEPS IN SAVE PROCEDURES]

3.4 Error Recovery

The following describes [PRODUCT NAME] error recovery procedures.
[STEPS IN ERROR RECOVERY PROCEDURES]

3.n [BASIC PROCEDURE NAME]

The following describes [PRODUCT NAME] [BASIC PROCEDURE NAME] procedures.
[STEPS IN BASIC PROCEDURE]

n. [TASK NAME]

This chapter describes [TASK NAME].
[TASK FUNCTIONAL DESCRIPTION,
INCLUDING ALL NECESSARY
COMMANDS AND PROCEDURES]

APPENDIX A—ERROR MESSAGES

This appendix lists and describes error messages.
   [LIST AND DESCRIPTION OF ERROR MESSAGES]

([APPENDIX TITLE]

This appendix contains [SUBJECT OF APPENDIX].
[TEXT OF APPENDIX])

GLOSSARY

The following terms and acronyms are used throughout [PRODUCT NAME] documentation.

      [LIST OF TERMS AND ACRONYMS
      AND THEIR DEFINITIONS]

(INDEX

[INDEX ENTRIES])

15 Release Description

1. **INTRODUCTION**
2. **INVENTORY**
3. **[FEATURES/ENHANCEMENTS]**
   3.n [FEATURE/ENHANCEMENT NAME]
4. **KNOWN PROBLEMS & WORKAROUNDS**
   4.n [PROBLEM AREA]
5. **INSTALLATION**
([APPENDIX])

1. INTRODUCTION

This Release Description describes [VERSION ID] of [PRODUCT NAME] in terms of:

1. The inventory of tape(s) and documentation.
2. The [FEATURES/ENHANCEMENTS] provided.
3. Known problems and their workarounds.
4. Installation procedures.

2. INVENTORY

The following lists the physical media and associated documentation that comprise ([VERSION ID]) of [PRODUCT NAME] (for [PLATFORM NAME]).

Medium:

[MEDIUM TYPE and NUMBER]

Documents:

[LIST OF DOCUMENTS]

(The following lists the physical media and associated documentation that comprise ([VERSION ID]) of [PRODUCT NAME] (for [PLATFORM NAME]).

Medium:

[MEDIUM TYPE and NUMBER]

Documents:

[LIST OF DOCUMENTS])

3. [FEATURES/ENHANCEMENTS]

The following features and enhancements are available with [VER-SION ID] of [PRODUCT NAME].
[INTRODUCTORY LIST OF
FEATURES/ENHANCEMENTS]

3.n [FEATURE/ENHANCEMENT NAME]

[FEATURE/ENHANCEMENT DESCRIPTION]

4. KNOWN PROBLEMS & WORKAROUNDS

The following are known problems and their workarounds. Fixes will be supplied as they become available.

4.n [PROBLEM AREA]

[PROBLEM DESCRIPTION]
[WORKAROUND DESCRIPTION]

5. INSTALLATION

The following procedures list the steps to install [SYSTEM NAME]
[VERSION NUMBER].
     [STEPS IN INSTALLATION PROCEDURE]

([APPENDIX TITLE]

This appendix contains [SUBJECT OF APPENDIX].
[TEXT OF APPENDIX])

16 System Administrators Guide

187

PREFACE

The following describes this system administrators guide in terms of purpose, audience, organization, and related documentation.

Purpose

This *[PRODUCT NAME] System Administrators Guide* provides information and procedures to set up [PRODUCT NAME] in its operational environment.

Audience

The intended users of this guide are system administrators (with [PRE-REQUISITE KNOWLEDGE]).

Organization

This guide describes [PRODUCT NAME] in terms of:
[DOCUMENT ORGANIZATION DESCRIPTION]

Documentation

Related documentation includes:
[LIST OF APPLICABLE DOCUMENTS]

COMMAND SYNTAX NOTATION

The following table lists and describes notation used throughout [PRODUCT NAME] publications to illustrate command syntax.

NOTATION	MEANING
[SYMBOL]	Required as shown
[SYMBOL]	Required
[SYMBOL]	Optional
[SYMBOL]	Choice
•••	Repeat
[SYMBOL]	[MEANING]

Examples:

SYNTAX: [COMMAND AS SHOWN IN GUIDE]
COMMAND: [COMMAND AS ENTERED BY USER]

SYNTAX: [COMMAND AS SHOWN IN GUIDE]
COMMAND: [COMMAND AS ENTERED BY USER]

NOTE: Any commands that do not conform to the above notation are identified in text.

1. INTRODUCTION

This chapter introduces [PRODUCT NAME] in terms of configuration(s), including hardware platforms, interfacing software, and network communications.
    [DESCRIPTION OF SYSTEM CONFIGURATION(S)]

2. SYSTEM SETUP

This chapter describes [PRODUCT NAME] system setup files in terms of purpose, contents, and example.

2.n [NAME] Setup File

Purpose:

[PURPOSE OF FILE]

Contents:

[CONTENTS OF FILE]

Example:

[EXAMPLE OF FILE]

3. NETWORK SERVICE SETUP

This chapter describes network service setup in terms of hardware and files.

3.1 Hardware

This section describes hardware network service setup in terms of cables and/or boards and switch settings.

[HARDWARE NETWORK SERVICE SETUP]

3.2 Files

The following subsections describe network service setup files in terms of purpose, contents, and example.

3.2.n [NAME] Network Service File

Purpose:

[PURPOSE OF FILE]

Contents:

[CONTENTS OF FILE]

Example:

[EXAMPLE OF FILE]

4. ACCOUNT ADMINISTRATION

This chapter describes [PRODUCT NAME] user account setup and maintenance in terms of account creation, modification, and deletion.

4.1 Account Creation

The following procedure creates a user account with the appropriate file protections/permissions.
    [STEPS IN ACCOUNT CREATION PROCEDURE]

4.2 Account Modification

The following procedure modifies an existing user account.
    [STEPS IN ACCOUNT MODIFICATION PROCEDURE]

4.3 Account Deletion

The following procedure deletes an existing user account.
    [STEPS IN ACCOUNT DELETION PROCEDURE]

5. PERIPHERALS

This chapter describes the software setup for peripherals supported by [PRODUCT NAME], including printers, plotters, and modems.

5.1 [NAME] Peripheral

The following subsections describe [PERIPHERAL NAME] in terms of models supported and files to be created or modified.

5.1.1 Models

[LIST OF MODELS SUPPORTED]

5.1.n [NAME] File

Purpose:

[PURPOSE OF FILE]

Contents:

[CONTENTS OF FILE]

Example:

[EXAMPLE OF FILE]

APPENDIX A — TROUBLESHOOTING

This appendix contains troubleshooting procedures described in terms of:

1. Symptom
2. Problem(s)
3. Solution(s)

Symptom:

   [DESCRIPTION OF SYMPTOM]

Problem:

   [DESCRIPTION OF POSSIBLE PROBLEM(S)]

Solution:

   [DESCRIPTION OF PROBABLE SOLUTION(S)]

([APPENDIX TITLE]

This appendix contains [SUBJECT OF APPENDIX].
[TEXT OF APPENDIX])

GLOSSARY

The following terms and acronyms are used throughout [PRODUCT NAME] documentation.

[LIST OF TERMS AND ACRONYMS
AND THEIR DEFINITIONS]

(INDEX

[INDEX ENTRIES])

17 Reference Guide

PREFACE

1. INTRODUCTION

2. [LANGUAGE NAME] CONSTRUCTS

3.   COMMAND DESCRIPTIONS
   3.n   [COMMAND NAME]
APPENDIX A — COMMAND SUMMARY
APPENDIX B — ERROR MESSAGES
([APPENDIX])
GLOSSARY
(INDEX)

PREFACE

The following describes this reference guide in terms of purpose, audience, organization, and related documentation.

Purpose

This *[PRODUCT NAME] Reference Guide* provides information and procedures for using [LANGUAGE NAME].

Audience

The intended users of this guide are [USER TITLES] (with [PREREQUISITE KNOWLEDGE]).

Organization

This guide describes [LANGUAGE NAME] in terms of:
　　　[DOCUMENT ORGANIZATION DESCRIPTION]

Documentation

Related documentation includes:
　　　[LIST OF APPLICABLE DOCUMENTS]

COMMAND SYNTAX NOTATION

The following table lists and describes notation used throughout [PRODUCT NAME] publications to illustrate command syntax.

NOTATION	MEANING
[SYMBOL]	Required as shown
[SYMBOL]	Required
[SYMBOL]	Optional
[SYMBOL]	Choice
•••	Repeat
[SYMBOL]	[MEANING]

Examples:

SYNTAX: [COMMAND AS SHOWN IN GUIDE]

COMMAND: [COMMAND AS ENTERED BY USER]

SYNTAX: [COMMAND AS SHOWN IN GUIDE]

COMMAND: [COMMAND AS ENTERED BY USER]

NOTE: Any commands that do not conform to the above notation are identified in text.

1. INTRODUCTION

This chapter introduces [LANGUAGE NAME] in terms of [USE(S)/ FEATURES DESCRIPTION].

2. [LANGUAGE NAME] CONSTRUCTS

This chapter describes [LANGUAGE NAME] constructs in terms of:

1. Syntax
2. Data types
3. Variables
4. Control structures
5. Macros
6. Error handling

2.1 Syntax

The following lists and describes notation used to illustrate [LANGUAGE NAME] command syntax. A copy of the Command Syntax Notation Table is included in the front matter of this guide.

NOTATION	MEANING
[SYMBOL]	Required as shown
[SYMBOL]	Required
[SYMBOL]	Optional
[SYMBOL]	Choice
•••	Repeat
[SYMBOL]	[MEANING]

The following subsections describe and exemplify syntax for:

1. Commands
2. Arguments
3. Operators
4. Function calls

5. Delimiters

6. Comments

2.1.1 Commands

The following describes the command types and methods of entry.
[COMMAND TYPE DESCRIPTIONS AND EXAMPLES]

2.1.2 Arguments

The following describes the argument types and methods of entry.
[ARGUMENT DESCRIPTIONS AND EXAMPLES]

2.1.3 Operators

The following describes the operator types and methods of entry.
[OPERATOR DESCRIPTIONS AND EXAMPLES]

2.1.4 Function Calls

The following describes function calls and returns.
[FUNCTION CALL DESCRIPTION AND EXAMPLES]

2.1.5 Delimiters

The following describes delimiter types and methods of entry.
[DELIMITER DESCRIPTIONS AND EXAMPLES]

2.1.6 Comments

The following describes the comment types and methods of entry.
[COMMENT DESCRIPTION AND EXAMPLES]

2.2 Data Types

The following subsections describe and exemplify data types in terms of:

1. Numbers
2. Strings
3. Lists
4. Named sets
5. Files

2.2.1 Numbers

The following types of numbers are supported.
[NUMBER DESCRIPTIONS AND EXAMPLES]

2.2.2 Strings

The following types of strings are supported.
[STRING DESCRIPTIONS AND EXAMPLES]

2.2.3 Lists

The following types of lists are supported.
[LIST DESCRIPTIONS AND EXAMPLES]

2.2.4 Named Sets

The following types of named sets are supported.
[NAMED SETS DESCRIPTIONS AND EXAMPLES]

2.2.5 Files

The following file formats are supported.
[FILE FORMAT DESCRIPTIONS AND EXAMPLES]

2.3 Variables

The following subsections describe variables in terms of their initialization and scope.

2.3.n [VARIABLE TYPE]

Initialization:

[VARIABLE INITIALIZATION DESCRIPTION AND EXAMPLES]

Scope:

[VARIABLE SCOPE DESCRIPTION AND EXAMPLES]

2.4 Control Structures

The following subsections describe and exemplify control structures.

2.4.n [CONTROL STRUCTURE]

[CONTROL STRUCTURE DESCRIPTION AND EXAMPLES]

2.5 Macros

The following subsections describe predefined macros and user-defined macros.

2.5.1 Predefined

[LIST AND DESCRIPTIONS OF PREDEFINED MACROS]

2.5.2 User-Defined

[PROCEDURE FOR CREATING USER-DEFINED MACROS]

2.6 Error Handling

The following describes error handling techniques.
[ERROR HANDLING TECHNIQUES DESCRIPTION]

3. COMMAND DESCRIPTIONS

This chapter lists each command in the [LANGUAGE NAME] command set and defines it in terms of syntax, description, and examples.

3.n [COMMAND NAME]

[SYNTAX]
[DESCRIPTION]
[EXAMPLE(S)]

APPENDIX A—COMMAND SUMMARY

This appendix contains an alphabetic summary of [LANGUAGE NAME] commands.
　　　[LIST OF COMMAND NAMES AND SYNTAX]

APPENDIX B — ERROR MESSAGES

This appendix lists error messages and describes them in terms of cause(s) and solution(s).

B.n [ERROR]

Cause(s):

[DESCRIPTION OF CAUSE(S)]

Solution(s):

[PROCEDURE FOR SOLUTION(S)]

([APPENDIX TITLE]

This appendix contains [SUBJECT OF APPENDIX].
[TEXT OF APPENDIX])

GLOSSARY

The following terms and acronyms are used throughout [PRODUCT NAME] documentation.

[LIST OF TERMS AND ACRONYMS
AND THEIR DEFINITIONS]

(INDEX

[INDEX ENTRIES])

18 Acceptance Signoff

1. SCOPE

The following describes this Acceptance Signoff in terms of its purpose and audience.

1.1 Purpose

This Acceptance Signoff provides information for performing [PRODUCT NAME] installation verification and acceptance.

1.2 Audience

The intended users of this Acceptance Signoff are the people responsible for [PRODUCT NAME] installation verification and acceptance.

2. INSTALLATION VERIFICATION TEST

The Installation Verification Test (IVT) verifies the proper loading and operation of the [PRODUCT NAME] System. The IVT program executes the following functions to verify the installation:
[LIST AND DESCRIPTION OF IVT FUNCTIONS]
(It is assumed that all other hardware and software have been installed and properly configured.)
The IVT will run for about [TIME DURATION].

2.1 Setting Up for the IVT

Perform the following setup for the IVT:
[STEPS IN SETUP PROCEDURE]

2.2 Executing the IVT

Execute the IVT by entering the following command(s):
[COMMAND(S) ENTRY PROCEDURE]

2.3 Checking for a Successful IVT

At the completion of the IVT, check the IVT logfile for errors and warnings. The log file is located in [LOCATION OF FILE].
If no errors are listed in the log file, then the IVT has completed successfully.
If errors are listed in the log file, then correct the errors and rerun the IVT.

3. [PRODUCT NAME] ACCEPTANCE

The following authorized signature(s) constitutes acceptance of the [PRODUCT NAME] System.

Company name & address

_____

_____

_____

Name:_____ Date:___/___/___

Title:_____

Name:_____ Date:___/___/___

Title:_____

A Basic Punctuation Rules

The following subset of punctuation rules will cover 99% of what you need to know about using:[56]

Periods	.
Commas	,
Colons	:
Semicolons	;
Apostrophes	'
Hyphens	-
Slashes	/
Parentheses	( )

PERIOD

1. Use a period to end every sentence.
2. Use a period at the end of a punctuated list that forms a sentence, for example:

   Use a period at the end of:
   1. **Imperative sentences,**
   2. **Declarative sentences, and**
   3. **Lists that form a sentence.**

COMMA

1. Use a comma before *and*, *or*, *nor*, *for*, *so*, *but*, and *yet* when they connect two parts that could each stand alone as a sentence (compound sentence).

2. Separate each element in a parallel series of three or more items by a comma, for example: **the x, the y, and the z inputs, or the x, y, and z inputs**—not "the x, the y and the z inputs"—unless you want the "y" and the "z" inputs to be considered as a set separate from the "x."

3. Set off introductory dependent clauses by a comma, for example: **When the file is opened, the message "Filename active" will appear at the top of the screen.**

4. Separate comparative structures with a comma, for example: **The faster the circuit, the more heat it generates.**

5. Set off contrasting words or phrases by a comma, for example: **The system is friendly, not clairvoyant.**

6. Use a comma to prevent misreading, for instance when words that often function as prepositions are used as adverbs, for example: **Beneath, the cables are connected to the winchester drives.**

7. Use commas to mark off three-number units in numbers containing four or more digits, for example: **2,851** and **18,371**.

COLON

Use a colon to introduce a series, a list, an explanation, an example, for example: **Parameters include: data widths, bus control signals, and cycle time.**

SEMICOLON

1. Use a semicolon to join two parts that could each stand alone as a sentence when no coordinating conjunction is used, for example: **The SAVE command writes the data to disk; the QUIT command does not.**

2. Use a semicolon before a conjunction that connects two parts that could each stand alone as a sentence, for example: **The RAM has 64 inputs; however, they do not all carry data.**

3. Use semicolons in a sentence that contains a series of clauses or phrases having internal commas, for example: **EXIT commands include FILE, which writes the data to disk; QUIT, which does not; and QQUIT, which gives you another chance.**

4. Use semicolons in a sentence that contains a series of numbers having internal commas, for example: **1,582; 170,040; and 17,381**.

APOSTROPHE

1. Use an apostrophe and an *s* to indicate possession in a singular noun, for example: **the instruction's second operand**.

2. Use an apostrophe to indicate possession in a plural noun that ends in an *s*, for example: **several instructions' operands**.

3. Only possessive acronyms take an apostrophe before the *s*; there is no apostrophe between an acronym and the plural *s*, for example:

    a. **CPUs = two or more.**

    b. **CPU's = belonging to one CPU.**

c. **CPUs'** = **belonging to more than one CPU.**

Note that the plural *s* following the acronym is lower case.

4. Do not use an apostrophe for the possessive pronoun *its*. *Its* is the same as *his* or *hers*.

HYPHEN

1. Hyphenate to form a compound adjective when the first word modifies the second, for examples: **low-intensity rays** and **high-performance CPU**.

2. Hyphenate multiple-word terms that precede a noun, for example: **two-to-one ratio**.

3. Hyphenate to prevent misreading, for instance between "re-creation" and "recreation."

4. Hyphenate a number-unit adjective, especially those involving bits, bytes, or pins, for examples: **64-bit bus, 16 KB block, 10-pin package**.

5. Hyphenate compound nouns naming a unit of measurement, for example: **foot-pound** and **kilowatt-hour**.

6. Hyphenate a mixed number between the integer and fraction, for example: **3-1/3**.

SLASH

1. Use a slash to mean "per" in a table, for example: **ops/sec**; but use the word "per" in the text, for example: **two minor cycles per cycle**.

2. Use a slash between two acronyms, for example: **CAD/CAM**.

PARENTHESES

1. Use parentheses to enclose an acronym the first time it's used (following the spelled out term), for example: **The Tower Control Sequencer (TCS)**. . . .

2. Use parentheses sparingly in text because they are often used as part of a command.

B Documentation Format Checklist

The following checklist provides fields in which you can specify the format for your documentation, including examples and templates of components that make up the front matter, back matter, and sections of your end-user documents.

FRONT MATTER

Page numbers:

    Lowercase Roman————
    Other————
    Example:

[EXAMPLE]

Front cover template:

[TEMPLATE]

Title page template:

[TEMPLATE]

Revision notice boilerplate:

[TEMPLATE]

Trademark notice templates:

Your company's trademarks:

[TEMPLATE(S)]

Other companies' trademarks:

[TEMPLATE(S)]

Copyright notice template:

[TEMPLATE]

Notation Table boilerplate:

[TEMPLATE]

Table of contents level_____

BACK MATTER

Appendix

Title designator:

Alpha_____
Roman_____
Other_____
Example:

[EXAMPLE]

Page numbers:

Prefaced by title designator———
Sequential by chapter———
Sequential through publication———
Example:

[EXAMPLE]

Glossary:

Optional———
Required———
Example:

[EXAMPLE FIRST PAGE]

Index:

Optional———
Required———
Example:

[EXAMPLE FIRST PAGE]

Back cover template:

[TEMPLATE]

SECTIONS

Page numbers:

Sequential throughout———
Prefixed with section number———
Example:

[EXAMPLE]

Running foot example:

[EXAMPLE]

Running head example:

[EXAMPLE]

Header levels:

1st level header example:

[EXAMPLE]

2nd level header example:

[EXAMPLE]

3rd level header example:

[EXAMPLE]

4th level header example:

[EXAMPLE]

5th level header example:

[EXAMPLE]

Paragraph limits:

maximum number of sentences_____
maximum number of lines_____

Warning example:

[EXAMPLE]

Caution example:

[EXAMPLE]

Note example:

[EXAMPLE]

Abbreviations:

IEEE Standard_____
Other [REFERENCE]_____

Symbols:

IEEE standard_____
Graphics system dependency_____
Other [REFERENCE]_____

List example:

[EXAMPLE]

Figures:

Always vertical_____
Horizontal allowed_____
Foldouts allowed_____
Figure caption example:

[EXAMPLE]

Tables:

Alignment of column heads:
Centered_____
Flush left_____
Alignment of entries:
Centered_____
Flush left_____
Table caption example:

[EXAMPLE]

Spelling List:

[ALPHABETIC LIST OF STANDARD SPELLING
FOR WORDS THAT COULD BE SPELLED,
HYPHENATED, OR CAPITALIZED IN
ALTERNATIVE WAYS]

C Acronyms and Abbreviations

Acronyms and abbreviations form a significant part of most technical documents. Standardizing their use can lead to both better documentation and better communication.

ACRONYMS

It's so much easier to read or talk about "MOSVLSI" than about "metal-oxide-semiconductor very large-scale integration" that acronyms have just about replaced many electronic terms. In fact, acronyms are so prevalent in the electronics industry that people often don't know the words the acronyms stand for.

Strictly speaking, an acronym is a construct that can be pronounced as a word, such as **ROM** (read only memory); and a group of letters pronounced as initials, such as **TTL** (transistor to transistor logic), is called an initialism. However, the distinction is fading, particularly because some acronyms may be pronounced either as a word or initials, such as **ALU** (arithmetic logic unit) and **EMA** (electromagnetic actuator); and others are a combination, such as **DRAM** (dynamic random access memory) and **CMOS** (complementary metal oxide semiconductor).

When you use an acronym:

1. Capitalize all letters in the acronym whether or not the words in the term are capitalized.
2. Put the acronym (in parentheses) immediately after the first use of the spelled out term.
3. Use the acronym consistently after it has been defined instead of switching back and forth between the acronym and the spelled out term.
4. Put all acronyms and their spelled out definitions in the glossary.

ABBREVIATIONS

An abbreviation is the shortened form of a word, composed of letters selected from the full word. Most abbreviations are not spoken, but some, such as **KB** (kilobyte) and **ac** (alternating current) are making acronyms even more difficult to define.

When you use an abbreviation:

1. If the first letter of the word is capitalized, then capitalize the first letter of the abbreviation.
2. Use the same abbreviation for a measure whether the amount is singular or plural, for example: **1 cm to 12 cm**.
3. Spell out *that is* (not "i.e.") and *for example* (not "e.g.") rather than abbreviating them.
4. Spell out *versus* (not "vs.").
5. Spell out *maximum* and *minimum* in text; abbreviate them to *max* and *min* in tables.
6. Don't use a period at the end of an abbreviation in a table.
7. Don't use a period at the end of an abbreviation in text unless the meaning would be ambiguous without it, for example, the preposition *in* and the measurement *in* (inch).

The IEEE and several Government agencies publish comprehensive lists of approved abbreviations. Table C–1 lists some of the more common.

Table C-1.   Common Abbreviations

A	ambient
A/D	analog to digital
c	centi- (hundredth)
cu	cubic
d	deci- (tenth)
D/A	digital to analog
da	deka- (ten)
dB	decibel
dc	direct current
G	giga- (billion)
GB	gigabyte
h	hecto- (hundred)
Hz	Hertz
ips	inches per second
IPS	instructions per second
k	kilo- (thousand)
K	kilo (1,024)
KB	kilobyte
M	mega- (million)
MB	megabyte
m	meter
m	milli- (thousandth)
n	nano- (billionth)
p	pico- (trillionth)
psi	pounds per square inch
s	second

REFERENCES

Introduction

1. Paula Bell, "The Politics of Technical Writing," *Computerworld*, February 16, 1987, 63–68.

2. Frederick P. Brooks, Jr., *The Mythical Man-Month*. Addison-Wesley Publishing Company, 2nd printing, 1978, 75.

3. Gerald M. Weinberg, *The Psychology of Computer Programming*. Van Nostrand Reinhold Company, 1971.

Part I

4. Frederick P. Brooks, Jr., "Essence and Accidents of Software Engineering," *Computer*, April 1987, 10–19.

5. Michael W. Evans, *The Software Factory*. John Wiley & Sons, Inc., 1989.

6. Walter Scacchi, Personal communication, November 1987.

Chapter 1

7. Paula Bell, "Think About It: A Cognitive Approach to Technical Writing," *Perspectives on Software Documentation: Inquiries and Innovations*, Baywood Publishing Company, Inc., in publication.

8. Evans, *Factory*.

9. Samuel C. Florman, *The Existential Pleasures of Engineering*, St. Martin's Press, 1976, 61.

10. Itzhak Shemer, "Systems Analysis: A Systematic Analysis of a Conceptual Model," *Communications of the ACM*, June 1987, 30, no. 6, 506–512.

11. Thomas J. Peters and Robert H. Waterman, Jr., *In Search of Excellence: Lessons from America's Best-Run Companies*. Harper & Row, Publishers, 1982, 30.

12. Russell L. Ackoff, *The Art of Problem Solving*. John Wiley & Sons, Inc., 1978, 76.

13. Peters & Waterman, Jr., *Search*, 39.

14. L. Bradford and Allan R. Cohen, *Managing for Excellence*, New York: John Wiley & Sons, Inc., 1984, 71.

15. David Hickey, "7 Principles To An Effective Engineering Environment," *Electronic Engineering Times*, Monday, July 6, 1987, 53–56.

16. Gerald M. Weinberg, *An Introduction to General Systems Thinking*. John Wiley & Sons, Inc., 1975, 21.

17. Christopher Alexander, *Notes on the Synthesis of Form*, Harvard University Press, ninth printing, 1977, 15–16.

18. John Zarella, *System Architecture*, Microcomputer Applications, 1980, 6–7.

19. Tor Guimarraes, "Prototyping, Orchestration For Success," *Datamation*, December 1, 1987, 101–106.

20. Tony Percy, "My Data, Right or Wrong," *Datamation*, June 1, 1986, 123–128.

21. Ronald A. Guillemette, "Prototyping: An Alternate Method for Developing Documentation," *Technical Communication*, Third Quarter 1987, 135–140.

22. Hassan Gomaa, "Software Development of Real-Time Systems," *Communications of the ACM*, 29, no. 7, July 1986, 657.

23. Michael W. Evans, *Productive Software Test Management*. John Wiley & Sons, Inc., 1984, 140.

24. Michael W. Evans, *Software Quality Assurance & Management*. John Wiley & Sons, Inc., 1987, 39–40.

25. Evans, *Test*, 164–165.

Chapter 2

26. Martin L. Rubin, *Documentation Standards and Procedures for Online Systems*. Van Nostrand Reinhold Company, 1979, xiv.

27. Paul D. Doebler, "Productivity Improvement Through Electronic Publishing," *Technical Communication*, Fourth Quarter, 1987, 250–256.

28. James H. Coombs, Allen H. Renear, and Steven DeRose, "Markup Systems and the Future of the Scholarly Text Processing," *Communications of the ACM*, 30, no. 11, November 1987.

29. Colette Daiuette, "The Computer as Stylus and Audience," *College Composition and Communication*, 34, no. 2, May 1983, 134–135.

30. John C. Bean, "Computerized Word-processing as an Aid to Revision," *College Composition and Communication* 34, no. 2, May 1983, 146–148.

31. Betsy A. Riley and Morris H. Slabbekorn, "Productivity Improvements Through Computer Graphics: A Case Study," *Technical Communication*, Fourth Quarter 1987, 257–263.

32. Sarah Calding, personal communication, December, 1987.

33. Lorinda L. Cherry, Lawrence T. Frase, Patricia S. Gingrich, Stacy A. Keenan, and Nina H. MacDonald, "Computer Aids for Text Analysis," *Bell Laboratories Record*, 61, no. 5, May/June 1983, 10–16.

34. F. W. Lancaster and Amy Warner, "Electronic Publication and Its Impact on the Presentation of Information," *The Technology of Text*, 2, Educational Technology Publications, 1985, 292–309.

35. Andrew Fluegelman and Jeremy John Hewes, *Writing in the Computer Age*, Anchor Books, Anchor/Doubleday, 1983, 225.

36. John B. Smith and Stephen F. Weiss, "Hypertext," *Communications of the ACM*, 31, no. 7, July 1988, 817.

Chapter 3

37. Michael W. Evans, Pamela Piazza, and James B. Dolkas, *Principles of Productive Software Management*, John Wiley & Sons, Inc., 58.

38. Richard Zaneski, *Software Manual Production Simplified*, Petrocelli Books, Inc., 1982, 13.

39. Martin Nystrand, *The Structure of Written Communication: Studies in Reciprocity Between Writers and Readers*, Academic Press, Inc., Harcourt Brace Jovanovich, Publishers, 1986, 87.

40. E. D. Hirsch, Jr., *Cultural Literacy*, Houghton Mifflin Company, 1987, 79.

41. R. John Brockmann, *Writing Better Computer User Documentation*, John Wiley & Sons, Inc., 1986, 198.

42. Christine Browning, *Guide to Effective Software Technical Writing*, Prentice-Hall, Inc., 95.

43. Gordon H. Mills and John A. Walter, *Technical Writing*, Holt, Rinehart and Winston, Inc., 1970, 216.

Chapter 4

44. Robert R. Blake, Jane S. Mouton, and Robert L. Allen, *Spectacular Teamwork*, John Wiley & Sons, Inc., 1987, 12.

45. Evans, Piazza, and Dolkas, *Management*, 69.

46. Brooks, Jr., *Man-Month*, 76.

47. Paula Bell, *HighTech Writing*, John Wiley & Sons, Inc., 1985, 167–172.

48. Hanna Bandes, "Designing and Controlling Documentation Quality—Part II," *Technical Communication*, Second Quarter 1987, 69–71.

49. Bell, *Politics*, 63–68.

50. Thomas T. Barker, "Feedback Mechanisms in Hightech Writing," *Journal of Technical Writing and Communication*, January 1988.

51. Browning, *Guide*, 49.

52. William Horton, "Quick Relief Documentation," *Proceedings of the International Technical Communications Conference*, May 1985.

53. John M. Carroll, "Minimalist Training," *Datamation*, November 1, 1984, 125–136.

54. Weinberg, *Programming*, 170.

55. Laurel N. Holder and Stephen P. O'Neill, "Editorial Authority and the Author: Who's in Control?" *Technical Communication*, First Quarter, 1987, 104.

Appendix A

56. Bell, *Writing*, 26.

GLOSSARY

The following words are used in the following ways in this book.

acceptance. Official transfer of a system to a customer.

Acceptance Signoff. A Document Master to be completed in the system delivery phase.

acceptance testing. Formal testing conducted to determine whether or not a system satisfies its acceptance criteria.

adaptation. The process of tailoring the Masters to your system specifications.

ADD. Architecture Design Document.

AI. Artificial Intelligence.

approval. Formal recognition of the validity and acceptability of an action or a product.

architectural design. Specification of the top-level functions, performance, and data flow of a system.

Architecture Design Document. A Document Master to be completed in the system development phase.

audit. An independent review for the purpose of assessing compliance with specifications, baselines, standards, procedures, or contractual and licensing agreements.

automation. The process of tailoring the Masters for computerized generation.

back matter. Material that appears in the back of a document, including appendix, glossary, and index.

baseline. A document or other product that has been reviewed, agreed upon, and that thereafter serves as the basis for advancement to the next phase of the life-cycle.

boilerplate. A template that is included without modification.

bottom-up. An approach that starts with the lowest level of a hierarchy and proceeds through progressively higher levels.

build. An operational version of software incorporating specific capabilities of the final system.

CAD. Computer aided design.

CAP. Computer aided publishing.

CASE. Computer aided software engineering.

CCB. Change Control Board.

change control. The process by which a change is proposed, evaluated, and resolved.

change control board. The authority responsible for evaluating and recommending disposition of proposed engineering changes and tracking implementation of the approved changes.

CISC. Complex instruction set computer.

component. A general term for a physical or part of a system or document.

configuration. The arrangement of a computer system or network as defined by its nature, number, and physical characteristics.

configuration item. A portion of a system that is designated for configuration management and therefore managed, developed, documented, and demonstrated according to established baselines.

configuration management. The process of identifying and defining the deliverable system items and controlling the release and change of these items throughout the system life-cycle.

contraction. The process of tailoring the Masters by combination and/or deletion.

cross reference. A reference to another part of a document or to another document.

DA. Design automation.

DDD. Detailed Design Document.

debugging. The process of identifying, analyzing, and correcting design defects.

DEC. Digital Equipment Corporation.

decomposition. The process of tailoring the Masters by separation into lower level documents.

design review. A formal meeting at which the design of a system is presented to a predesignated panel for inspection, comment, and approval.

Detailed Design Document. A Document Master to be completed in the system development phase.

DID. Data Item Description.

Document Master. One of a set of document outlines provided as a guideline for system documentation from concept to delivery. The Document Masters are contained in Parts II through V of this book.

documentation. All written and illustrative information specifying, describing, reporting, or certifying requirements, designs, procedures, or results during the life-cycle.

documentation control. The process of defining and tracking documentation throughout the life-cycle.

DoD. Department of Defense.

driver file. A computer file that contains commands to call and include other files.

ECP. Engineering Change Proposal.

editor. An application that allows text entry, modification, and storage.

Engineering Change Proposal. A Document Master to be completed in the project control structuring phase and used throughout the life-cycle as the official request and validation of any changes that will influence the development and/or delivery of the system.

error. A discrepancy between an observed condition and the specified or theoretically correct condition.

FCS. First customer ship.

fog index. An algorithm that counts occurrences of syllables in a word and words in a sentence.

format. The arrangement of a document, including components, page layout, and type fonts.

formatter. An application that specifies the format of a document.

front matter. Material that appears at the front of a document, including title page, trademark notices, copyright notice, notation table, and table of contents.

hardware. Physical equipment used in data processing.

hypermedia. A software package that creates cross referenced information that includes text, graphics, audio, and video.

hypertext. A software package that creates cross referenced text and graphics.

integration. 1. The process of combining system components into a complete system. 2. The process of tailoring the Masters by merging them with an existing organization or set of documents.

integration testing. The progression of tests in which system components are combined and tested until the complete system has been tested.

interface. A shared boundary for interaction with another system component.

IVT. Installation verification test.

life-cycle. The period of time that starts when a software product is specified and ends when the product is no longer available for use.

maintainability. A given period of time in which a component under stated conditions of use can be restored to a state in which it can perform its required functions.

Management Plan. A Document Master to be completed in the project control structuring phase.

marketeer. Synonymous with *marketing analyst* and *marketer*.

Master. See Document Master.

milestone. A scheduled event used to measure progress, for example, a specification issuance, a phase review, product delivery.

MIPS. Million instructions per second.

module. An aggregate of related units.

MP. Management Plan.

MSI. Medium scale integration.

N/A. Not applicable.

operational testing. Testing performed on software in its normal operating environment.

PDD. Prototype Design Document.

protocols. A set of rules or procedures.

prototype. Software incorporating or exemplifying specific capabilities of the system under development.

Prototype Design Document. A Document Master to be completed in the system development phase.

quality. The degree to which the system or part of the system is able to perform its specified use.

Reference Guide. A Document Master to be completed in the system delivery phase.

regression testing. Selective retesting to detect faults introduced during modification of a system or system component.

Release Description. A Document Master to be completed in the system delivery phase.

reliability. The ability to perform a required function under stated conditions for a stated period of time.

Resource Requirements Specification. A Document Master produced in the requirements specification phase.

RISC. Reduced instruction set computer.

roff. runoff, a formatter originally designed at Bell Laboratories.

RRS. Resource Requirements Specification.

simulator. A device, data processing system, or computer program that represents specific features of the behavior of a physical or abstract system.

software development. The time that begins with the approval to develop or modify a software product and ends when the product is transferred to operational status.

spell checker. A software application that checks word spelling in a file.

SRS. System Requirements Specification.

style checker. An application that checks for grammar and syntax in a text file.

system. A group of components functioning as a single unit to accomplish a set of specific functions.

System Administrators Guide. A Document Master to be completed in the system delivery phase.

System Requirements Specification. A Document Master to be completed in the requirements specification phase.

template. A pattern used to shape a part of a document.

test case. A specified set of data and procedures developed to test system or subsystem compliance with a specific requirement.

test level. A range of tests in which the lowest level is a unit test and the highest level is a test of the system in its operational environment.

Test Log. A document describing the conduct and results of the testing carried out for a system or system component.

test procedure. Instructions for the setup, operation, data gathering, and evaluation of results for a given test.

Test Reports. A Document Master to be completed in the system development phase.

Test Specifications. A Document Master to be completed in the system development phase.

testability. The extent to which the evaluation of a system can be achieved.

testing. The process of exercising and evaluating a system or system component to verify that it satisfies specifications.

text processing. Computer manipulation of character strings.

top-down. An approach that starts with the highest level components in a hierarchy and proceeds through progressively lower levels.

TR. Test Reports.

traceability. The extent to which information exists in one document that leads to its precedent or antecedent in another.

TS. Test Specifications.

unit. The lowest standalone part of a program handled as a single entity.

Users Guide. A Document Master to be completed in the system delivery phase.

verification. The process of determining whether or not the product of a given phase fulfills its requirements.

wordprocessor. A combination editor and formatter.

WYSIWYG. What you see is what you get.

INDEX